Don Quixote

James Fenton was born in Lincoln in 1949 and educated at Magdalen College, Oxford, where he won the Newdigate Prize for poetry. He has worked as political journalist, drama critic, book reviewer, war correspondent, foreign correspondent and columnist. He is a Fellow of the Royal Society of Literature and was Oxford Professor of Poetry for the period 1994–99. His poetry collections include *Children in Exile* and *Out of Danger*, for which he was awarded the Whitbread Prize. He wrote libretti for *Haroun and the Sea of Stories* (New York City Opera) and *Tsunami Song Cycle* (BBC Symphony Orchestra) and his theatre includes *Pictures from an Exhibition* (Young Vic), *Tamar's Revenge* and *The Orphan of Zhao* (both Royal Shakespeare Company). In 2007 he was awarded the Queen's Gold Medal for Poetry and, in 2015, the PEN/Pinter prize. He is editor of *The New Faber Book of Love Poems*. *Yellow Tulips: Poems 1968–2011* was published by Faber and Faber in 2012.

by James Fenton from Faber

YELLOW TULIPS: POEMS 1968–2011

THE LOVE BOMB AND OTHER MUSICAL PIECES

THE NEW FABER BOOK OF LOVE POEMS

WILLIAM BLAKE: POET TO POET

SAMUEL TAYLOR COLERIDGE

CAMBODIAN WITNESS
The Autobiography of Someth May
(*editor*)

THE ORPHAN OF ZHAO

JAMES FENTON

Don Quixote

*a play with songs adapted from
the novel by Miguel de Cervantes Saavedra
as translated by Charles Jarvis*

FABER & FABER

First published in 2016
by Faber and Faber Limited
74–77 Great Russell Street
London WC1B 3DA

Typeset by Country Setting, Kingsdown, Kent CT14 8ES
Printed and bound by CPI Group (UK) Ltd, Croydon CR0 4YY

A CIP record for this book
is available from the British Library

ISBN 978–0–571–33158–1

Don Quixote was first presented by the Royal Shakespeare
Company at the Swan Theatre, Stratford-upon-Avon,
on 25 February 2016. The play premiered on 3 March
2016. The cast was as follows:

A VILLAGE IN LA MANCHA

Don Quixote David Threlfall
Sancho Panza Rufus Hound

Niece of Don Quixote Rosa Robson
Housekeeper Amy Rockson
Boy Richard Leeming
Teresa Panza Gemma Goggin
Priest Nicholas Lumley
Barber Timothy Speyer

ON THE ROAD

Innkeeper John Cummins
Sowgelder Natey Jones
Merchants Tom McCall, Theo Fraser Steele,
    Eleanor Wyld
Monks Richard Leeming, Timothy Speyer
Biscayan Gabriel Fleary
Shepherds Gemma Goggin, Natey Jones, Tom McCall,
    Timothy Speyer
Marcela Eleanor Wyld
Travelling Barber Will Bliss
Gines de Pasamonte Theo Fraser Steele
Galley Slaves Ruth Everett, Gabriel Fleary
Guards Tom McCall, Rosa Robson

Samson Carrasco Joshua McCord
Peasant Woman Eleanor Wyld
Acrobats Natey Jones, Tom McCall
Devil Nicholas Lumley
Lion Keeper John Cummins
Duchess Ruth Everett
Duke Theo Fraser Steele
Savage Gabriel Fleary
Physician Tom McCall
Steward Will Bliss
Soldier Natey Jones
Altisidora Bathsheba Piepe
Emerencia Amy Rockson

All other parts played by members of the company

Director Angus Jackson
Designer Robert Innes Hopkins
Lighting Designer Johanna Town
Composer and Co-Orchestrator Grant Olding
Sound Designer Jeremy Dunn
Comedy Director Cal McCrystal
Movement Director Lucy Cullingford
Puppetry Designer and Co-Director Toby Olié

Characters

Don Quixote de La Mancha
Sancho Panza
Teresa Panza
Barber
Priest
Boy
Niece
Housekeeper

Sowgelder
Innkeeper
A Biscayan
Marcela
Gines de Pasamonte
Samson Carrasco
Lion-Keeper
Duke *and* Duchess
Physician
Altisidora *and* Emerencia

Women, Carriers, Merchants, Monks, Ladies,
Shepherds, Galley Slaves, Guards, Actors, Courtiers

Songs, Poems, Musical Numbers

1 *The Ballad of the Raven*
   (Sancho Panza)

2 *The Song of the Quest*
   (Don Quixote)

3 *I Was Born with a Stain on my Chin*
   (Sowgelder)

4 *The Soldier Limping Down the Track*
   (Sancho Panza)

5 *Benedictine Monk Music*
   (Company)

6 *The Age of Gold*
   (Sancho and Don Quixote)

7 *Beauty is Cruel*
   (Don Quixote)

8 *Oh Run to the Door*
   (Galley Slaves)

9 *The Devil a Farthing to Pay*
   (Company)

10 *Wake Now*
   (Niece)

11 *Death the Acrobat*
   (Company)

12 *The Night Comes Down Like a Cloak*

13 *The Watcher in the Square*

14 *Go Home, Old Man*
   (Samson)

15 *Sancho's Epilogue*

16 *Final Dance*

DON QUIXOTE

ACT ONE

1 At the Barber's
2 Sancho Panza Sets the Scene
3 Don Quixote Arms Himself
4 At the Inn
5 On the Road
6 Back in the Village
7 The Return of Don Quixote
8 The Burning of the Books
9 The Disappearing Library
10 Don Quixote Proposes to Sancho Panza
11 The Adventure of the Windmills
12 The Fight with the Biscayan
13 A Question of Food
14 Marcela and Chrysostom
15 Don Quixote and the Sheep
16 The Helmet of Mambrino
17 Don Quixote and the Chain Gang
18 The Madness of Don Quixote
19 The Homecoming

ACT TWO

1 Don Quixote Asleep
2 The Return of Sancho
3 Enter a Wag
4 The Parliament of Death
5 Visiting Toboso
6 The Knight of the Mirrors
7 The Knight and the Lions
8 Enter a Duchess
9 Sancho's Government
10 Don Quixote Alone and Altisidora
11 Don Quixote Reunited with Sancho Panza
12 The Defeat of Don Quixote
13 The Deathbed

Act One

A village in La Mancha. At the barber's, Alonso Quixano (later to be called Don Quixote) is having a trim. The priest is waiting his turn. Sancho Panza is in attendance, ready to sweep up or perform any task for a tip. Sancho sings to himself.

The Ballad of the Raven

Sancho Panza
O take the arrow from your bow.
Point it not to the sky.
And do not shoot that royal bird.
King Arthur did not die.

The king was charmed by Merlin's art
When his heart broke for woe.
King Arthur flew from Camelot,
A raven black as the sloe.

The king flew from the English land
Until he came to a plain.
He saw a knight beneath a tree
Under the sun of Spain.

Look up, Sir Lancelot, look up
Look up into the tree.
I Arthur am, your raven king,
And you were false to me.
I Arthur am, your raven king,
And you were false to me.

I am not dead, the raven said.
I shall be king again.

3

But you shall die and you shall lie
Under the sun of Spain,
The sun of Spain.

Don Quixote That song again. Give that man an escudo on my account, Master Nicholas. It never ceases to amaze me that an ignorant man such as this, a peasant who can probably scarcely spell his name, should be possessed of such a rich store of learning. Where does it come from?

Priest These old ballads are the memory of the people. Without them we would forget who we are.

Don Quixote And it is true what the song says. Sir Lancelot did come to Spain. And from that time the order of chivalry has spread throughout the world, although, to tell the truth, we now live in a degenerate age. When was the last time you saw a knight who would sleep out in the open field, exposed to the rigour of the heavens, in a complete set of armour from head to foot? Someone who would ride all day through the forest, climb a mountain, find himself at the barren shore of the sea –

Priest A sea at the top of a mountain?

Don Quixote – and on that deserted beach, a small boat, a skiff, no oars, no mast, no sail or tackle of any kind, but a true knight doesn't wait to be told. Boldly he throws himself into the boat and pushes off –

Barber Pushes off with . . . ?

Priest With his lance.

Don Quixote – exposing himself to the implacable billows of the profound sea, which throw him up into the sky, then down into the abyss. Eager for adventure, he leaps from the boat on to the remote and unknown shore. And there he performs such deeds –

Barber What I've never understood, Alonso, is – these knights errant, these heroes you talk about from four hundred years ago, what deeds did they do?

Don Quixote What deeds did they do? What kind of question is that?

Barber They wandered.

Don Quixote They wandered, but they wandered to a purpose, which was to put themselves in danger's way, to fight injustice, and to burnish their honour thereby. And that's a trait that I seem to have inherited from them. Set me down in mid-field against a dozen fire-breathing warriors – giants, if you please – and I – I, Don Quixote de la Mancha, will show you what stuff of I am made of!

Priest *and* **Barber** Don Quixote de La Mancha?

Barber This is new.

Priest It may be his books have pushed him over the edge.

Don Quixote Don Quixote de La Mancha, the flower, the epitome of Spanish nobility, a byword for knightly virtue and grace. A man with a quest to bring back the age of chivalry in Spain.

The Song of the Quest

I see their tents pitched far on the horizon.
I hear their horses thunder across the plain.
Where are the kings and where the lords in waiting?
Bring back the age of chivalry to Spain.

Bring me a breastplate, beaten, chased and gilded.
Fetch me a lance of perfect weight and true.
Find me the finest sword in all Toledo.
Tempered seven times in morning dew.

I hear the wind blow through their fine pavilions.
I see their favours trampled in the rain.

Where are the queens and all the knights who
  loved them?
Bring back the age of chivalry to Spain.

Master Nicholas, I thank you for the toilette, which you
may chalk up to my account. Come, Señor Pero Perez,
you shall dine with me. It is a modest table I keep, yet for
all that . . .

SCENE TWO
SANCHO PANZA SETS THE SCENE

Sancho Panza 'It is a modest table I keep'! Little boiled
bits of this and that, and the leftovers come back cold in
the evening. Lentils on Fridays. On Sundays, with luck, a
small pigeon. And that accounts for three-quarters of his
income.

His family? One housekeeper, a niece and a lad for the
field and the market – it's not an impressive establishment.
It's what you might call the *residue* of an estate. He sold
off his best fields long ago to raise money for his hefty
great books on knights errants and damsels in distress.
And at times when he is idle – by which I mean the greatest
part of the year – you can often see him at his window
book in hand, dreaming of monsters to kill. Somewhere
in the dark depths of his house there's a rack on the wall,
and on that rack an old lance, gathering dust.

We're all gathering dust here.

Amazing things, books. I mean, what amazing things
they must be. This gentleman, this barber and this priest
never stop going on about them. They've got nothing else
to do. None of us has very much to do. Nothing much
happens here in this bit of La Mancha, in this village
without a name.

It's funny how, for the rest of us, life seems to pass in a
trance. I look at the road, that little trail of white. It loses

6

itself in the hills. But then it reappears, further up, thinner and paler, like a tailor's mark in chalk. I know the exact spot on the horizon where the sun rises in winter, and where it sinks on the longest day. I know every tree in the landscape. Every pasture, every peak. What lies beyond I do not know.

Teresa Panza Sancho. Sancho!

Sancho Panza That's the wife, by the way, a very good woman.

A very good woman.

SCENE THREE
DON QUIXOTE ARMS HIMSELF

Don Quixote at home, among some rusting pieces of armour. His Boy is assisting in the cleaning and repairing of it.

Don Quixote This, boy, this was the helmet of no less a man than my great-great-grandfather, Don Alvaro, and little did he suspect that his great-great-grandson would be crowned Emperor of Trebizond for the valour of his arms. Emperor of Trebizond! Me!

Boy Emperor of Trebizond?

Don Quixote It's only a matter of time! Now, observe this. No knight can last an instant in the field without his helmet. It is his trustiest friend and, next to his sword, his closest companion.

Every knight requires a mistress to inspire his deeds of valour.

A peasant girl walks across the stage

Aldonza Lorenzo. I loved her once, from afar. I never told her of my love I kept all my sorrows safe in my study, locked up like title deeds.

What if, instead of Aldonza Lorenzo, I were to choose a slightly more imposing-sounding name . . . the Lady Dulcinea del Toboso?

I, Don Quixote de La Mancha, do love and serve her, the lady Dulcinea del Toboso.

Fetch me the famous steed of Don Quixote! For, to be sure, just as Alexander had his Bucephalus, and El Cid had his Babieca, so the future Emperor of Trebizond, Don Quixote de La Mancha, must have his . . . his Rosinante!

Boy Rosinante?

The Boy has returned with an old wreck of a horse.

Your horse, sir.

Don Quixote My *steed*! The faithful companion of my exploits. Help me up, boy. Now hand me my helmet first, and now my shield . . . and now my lance. I thank you.

In future times, when the faithful history of my famous exploits comes to light, my first adventure will begin like this: 'Scarcely had the ruddy Phoebus spread his golden tresses over the wide and spacious earth . . . when the renownèd Don Quixote de La Mancha, abandoning the lazy down of a feathered bed – feathered bed? featherèd bed – mounted his famous courser –' That's you, Rosinante, oho!

The horse rears proudly. Don Quixote keeps his balance with some difficulty.

Boy Shall I open the gate, sir?

Don Quixote Open the gate! Open the gate indeed! Let the adventure begin. Rosinante! Oh no!

The horse rears. The Boy opens the gate. The Priest, the Barber and Sancho Panza watch the difficult departure of Don Quixote.

Barber 'And thus our flaming adventurer set forth.'

Priest Who would have thought a man could be so foolish?

Sancho Panza Foolish maybe, but still – a quest is a quest.

Barber You sound as if you envy him his exploits, Sancho Panza. Don't fret about it. He'll be back.

Priest Let's hope so.

Sancho Panza He'll be back, and we'll all still be here, God willing. The difference is, he will have lived, while we will have gone to seed.

Voice of Teresa Panza Sancho.

Sancho Panza That's my wife, by the way.

Voice of Teresa Panza Sancho!

Sancho Panza A very good woman.

SCENE FOUR
AT THE INN

Don Quixote is riding along on Rosinante.

I was Born with a Stain on my Chin

Sowgelder
I was born with a stain on my chin.
I was born to the stench of a sty.
My mother said, 'Son you were fathered in sin.'
My father said, 'Boy you were born in a bin
And you'd better get used to the mess you are in.'
Look at life through a sowgelder's eye –
Good or bad –
Look at life through a sowgelder's eye

9

So they taught me the sowgelder's art
And they set me to work with the swine
At a simple procedure involving a part
Where a single incision is certain to smart.
When it comes to pursuing affairs of the heart
I'm just glad that they left me with mine –
Good or bad –
I'm relieved that they left me with mine.

When the women come out on the street
At the sound of the sowgelder's horn
And I see something sharp in the eyes that I greet
And I drop them a word they would blush to repeat
And they mention a place and a time we could meet –
Should I wish that I'd never been born? –
Good or bad –
Should I wish that I'd never been born?

Don Quixote Now what is this apparition? It is a castle, as ever I live – a castle with four turrets, battlements of refulgent silver, with a drawbridge and a deep moat. The sort of castle where a man could well be dubbed a knight, according to ancient dubbing ceremonies of yore. Halt awhile, Rosinante. In a moment, a dwarf will appear on the battlements, and trumpets will announce the arrival of this wandering knight.

Don Quixote begins to put on his helmet.

Woman What have we here?

Don Quixote Fly not, ladies, nor fear any discourtesy, for the order of knighthood, which I profess permits me not to offer injury to anyone much less to virgins of such high rank as your presence denotes

Innkeeper Señor, if your worship is in quest of a lodging, we have everything you need – food, wine, a place by the fire.

Don Quixote I am impressed by the humility of the governor of this fortress, and his respectful mien. Any space will serve me. 'Arms are my ornament and fighting is my repose.'

Innkeeper I don't want any trouble now. Sir, let me help you off this . . . this . . .

Don Quixote This steed of mine.

Innkeeper May I help you dismount?

Don Quixote I hear music.

Innkeeper I'll tell the sowgelder to pipe down.

Don Quixote No, it's perfect. The castle was enchanted with the softest of melodies.
    Señor, I have a boon to ask of you. I would have you dub me a knight.

Innkeeper Dub you a knight?

Don Quixote Tonight, like the knights of yore, I shall watch over my arms in the chapel of your castle –

Innkeeper Chapel of my castle.

Don Quixote – and thereafter you shall dub me a knight, that I may be qualified to wander the four quarters of the world, in quest of adventures.

Innkeeper And may I inquire if you have any money about you?

Don Quixote Not a farthing! How strange you should ask this. For never in all the histories of knights errant have I ever read of a knight carrying money.

Innkeeper You know, the romances may not mention such details, but the knights of old always carried money and they always carried, in a little fardel . . . a change of clothes, and ointments and bandages for their wounds . . .

Don Quixote Bandages!

Innkeeper Or if they did not, they had *squires* to carry these things.

Don Quixote He's right, upon my soul. How could I have forgotten? I set out on my adventures without a squire!

Innkeeper There's no chapel here at present. It's being rebuilt. But you can watch your armour here in this font and later I'll give you the dubbing you deserve and send you on your way. (*To the Carriers, women and other guests.*) Watch out for him. He's as mad as a March hare. He's going to 'keep vigil over his armour' here . And later he wants to be knighted.

> *Don Quixote stacks his armour around the horse trough and kneels to keep his vigil.*
> *Cock-crow. The Sowgelder approaches the trough in order to water his mule.*

Don Quixote Ho, there, whoever thou art, rash knight that approachest to touch the arms of the most valorous adventurer that ever girded sword, take heed what thou doest and touch them not!

Sowgelder Get lost and take this junk with you. I've got my mule to water.

Don Quixote Assist me now, Dulcinea del Toboso, let not thy favour and protection fail me in this moment of danger.

> *Lifts his lance and strikes the Sowgelder very hard.*

Sowgelder What the –

Innkeeper I warned you, brother sowgelder, he's quite mad.

Sowgelder He's dangerous. You see what he did? Look at that. He could have killed me.

Carriers Go for him, Pablito. Teach him a lesson. Go for his nuts.

They start pelting Don Quixote with anything that comes to hand.

Innkeeper He'll kill the lot of you. I've seen madmen like this.

Don Quixote You are a false and base-born knight, to suffer a knight errant to be treated like this. I'll make you smart for your treachery. And you, you scoundrels, come on and do your worst. You'll see the reward you get.

Innkeeper Calm down, everyone.

Sir, I apologise for this insult to your person. But see – (*Producing large accounts book.*) I have here the order of ceremony for your dubbing. Let us proceed without delay. Kneel before me.

He chants plausibly.

Veritas veritatum.
Eliminans peccatum.
Heliogabalus. Amen.

The Innkeeper gives Don Quixote a blow.

Arise, Don Quixote de La Mancha. Now, my dear, give the knight his sword.

First Woman God make you a fortunate knight and give you success in battle.

Innkeeper Go forth into the world!

Sowgelder And good riddance.

Don Quixote 'Go forth into the world and good quittance.' It was a noble wish, nobly expressed. I have been dubbed a knight. And yet I have also been forced to admit that there is something missing. I set out on my adventures without a squire to assist me.

A group of Merchants with servants and umbrellas.

Halt there, gentlemen, and confess that there is not in the whole world a damsel more beautiful than Lady Dulcinea del Toboso. Halt, I say.

First Merchant Señor Cavalier, we do not know who this good lady may be. Let us see her. If she is as great a beauty as you say, we will, of course, acknowledge that fact.

Don Quixote If I showed her to you, what would be the merit in confessing such an obvious truth? No. The point is that without seeing her you believe, confess, affirm and swear that what I say is true.

Second Merchant And if not?

Don Quixote If not, I challenge you all to battle, proud and monstrous as you are.

Merchants Hey, wait a minute, that can't be right. What is this?

Don Quixote You can fight me one by one, as the laws of chivalry require, or altogether. Either way we must fight.

First Merchant Show us her portrait if we may not see the original. We don't doubt your word, and I'm sure we shall easily be convinced of her beauty, even if she has a squint.

Don Quixote A squint, eh? You shall pay for that blasphemy. Assist me, Lady Dulcinea.

Don Quixote charges at the First Merchant, his lance at the ready. But Rosinante falls, and the Don is left lying on his back, unable to move. The Merchants begin to disperse.

Fly not, you dastardly rabble. It is my horse's fault, not my own, that I lie here extended.

SCENE SIX
BACK IN THE VILLAGE

The Soldier Limping Down the Track

Sancho Panza
The soldier limping down the track,
The pilgrim at the inn –
Each bears a story on his back.
Each has a yarn to spin.

One travels with a seething heart.
One comes from fearful wars.
Give them some wine. They'll show their wounds
By firelight, by the stars.

They talk the blazing night away.
The wine – it suits them well.
They never ask a thing of me.
I have no tale to tell.

South – the stars of Africa.
North – the lands that freeze.
I never trod those frozen tracks
Nor crossed those boiling seas.

They talk the blazing night away.
I listen as I lie.

The moon looks down and laughs at me
And the stars burn in the sky.

The moon sticks out its tongue at me
And the stars burn in the sky.

SCENE SEVEN
THE RETURN OF DON QUIXOTE

*At Don Quixote's house. Priest, Barber, Niece,
Housekeeper.*

Don Quixote Be gentle now. My wounds are deep.

Barber My dear old friend. Where exactly are you
wounded?

Don Quixote Ten giants. It was a lusty combat.

Barber I see no wounds yet. But you are badly bruised.

Don Quixote Bear me to my chamber and summon the
priest. I shall shortly break bread with the immortals.

Priest My dear friend, surely you recognise . . .

Don Quixote You are a priest. Something tells me you
are a priest. Oh, shrive me, shrive me.

Priest I can't shrive you just like that.

Barber Why not? He might peg out at any moment. You
can't let him die unshriven.

Priest I don't have my shriving-things.

Barber Call yourself a priest and you don't have your
shriving-things? When was the last time you shrove
anyone? Think hard. There's a man here who might very
well be bleeding to death and who very likely has blood
on his hands.

Don Quixote Twenty giants. It was a fearsome struggle.

Niece This is what books did. I'll never forgive them.

Sancho Panza and the Boy carry Don Quixote off to his bedroom.

SCENE EIGHT
THE BURNING OF THE BOOKS

Housekeeper, Priest and Barber in Don Quixote's study. The Housekeeper brings a vessel of holy water and a bunch of hyssop. They are sorting through the books.

Housekeeper Romances everywhere – there must be a hundred of them. Reverend Father, I've brought some holy water here so you can exorcise them.

Priest Thank you. Let's see what he's got here. Chivalry, chivalry, chivalry. Out. Out. Out. You can chuck them down into the yard and we'll make a bonfire of them, while he's asleep.

Barber *The Adventure of Queen Pintiquiniestra with the Shepherd Darinel.* Dreadful. *Florismarte of Hyrcania* – appalling style – out he goes. *The Mastiff and the Damsel Plazedemivida* – sounds filthy.

Niece There's poetry over there.

Priest Maybe we should leave it.

Housekeeper Oh no, whatever you do, don't leave the poetry. The next thing he'll be turning into a shepherd and piping away in the fields. Burn the lot I say.

Priest Right you are. Out goes all the poetry.

Barber Meanwhile the best thing would be to brick up the study and make it look as if it's never been there. That way you'll removed the source of the mischief.

Priest He must have a lot of sleep to catch up on.

SCENE NINE
THE DISAPPEARING LIBRARY

While the Priest and the Barber block up the library, the Niece is tending to Don Quixote in his chamber. The Housekeeper and Sancho Panza later.

Don Quixote Help me up. I want to visit my library. There's a book there that has been much on my mind: *The Etiquette and Training of the Squire.*

Niece I'm sure you should just be resting.

Don Quixote Why, I must be going mad. I can't find my way around my own house.

Niece Do go back to bed, Uncle. You'll only distress yourself.

Don Quixote starts feeling his way along the wall, trying to find the missing study which has been bricked and plastered over.

Don Quixote Where is my study, my book room?

Niece Oh dear.

Housekeeper There are no books in this house. The Devil carried them all away.

Niece No, it was some kind of Enchanter. He went into the room and flew out through the roof, cackling to himself riding on a serpent. The room and all the books had vanished. Said his name was Munaton.

Don Quixote Friston, he meant to say.

Niece It definitely ended in -ton.

Don Quixote It does indeed. He is a cunning enchanter and a great enemy of mine. My beautiful library, all my books, vanished. It gives me unbearable, inexpressible grief.

Housekeeper Here's Sancho Panza, sir. You calm him down and mind you don't mention you know what.

Sancho Panza (*scratching his head*) You know what? Oh, *you* know what!

SCENE TEN
DON QUIXOTE PROPOSES TO SANCHO PANZA

Don Quixote It was brought home to me, S—

Sancho Panza Sancho.

Don Quixote Sancho . . . Panza, rather forcefully, on my latest adventure – do you have a fardel?

Sancho Panza A fardel?

Don Quixote It was pointed out to me, rather, as I say, forcefully, that a knight in my position should never set forth on his adventures without some kind of fardel, and in that fardel some trifling sum of money for his expenses on the journey, and some bandages and ointments or salves for his wounds (if any) and some – what was the other thing?

Sancho Panza Soap?

Don Quixote No, I don't think soap came into it.

Sancho Panza Some cheese, I should say, and a couple of onions to munch on in between adventures. A few dried figs always seem to hit the spot.

Don Quixote No, it was something else.

Sancho Panza Raisins are good. Wine of course.

Don Quixote No, it was – ah yes, a clean shirt.

Sancho Panza And you thought to yourself, I wonder if Sancho Panza has such a fardel.

Don Quixote No, no, no. It was also pointed out, and I could see the force of the argument, that a knight in my position should have a squire.

Sancho Panza You mean I should be your . . . I should be your squire.

Don Quixote And carry the fardel, and accompany me on my adventures, killing dragons, humiliating giants and rescuing damsels in distress.

Sancho Panza This is utterly and completely impossible.

Don Quixote Your reluctance does you credit. It would be a great undertaking, fit only for the fearless. But you must know, Sancho Panza, my dear friend –

Sancho Panza 'My dear friend', he says . . .

Don Quixote – that it was the custom among knights errant of old to make their squires governors of the islands or kingdoms they conquered. I'm determined that such a laudable old practice should not fall into desuetude.

Sancho Panza No indeed. I detest desuetude.
So then, if I became King of an island, by one of these miracles you mention, my children would be Infantas and Teresa Panza, my better half, my crooked rib, would become Queen.

Don Quixote Who doubts it, my dear Sancho Panza – who doubts it?

Sancho Panza I doubt it. She's not worth two farthings for a queen, if you must know. She's a very good woman, as I always say, but she has limitations. Mind you, if she were a countess, or a duchess even, that I could perhaps see.

Don Quixote My dear Sancho Panza, don't be too modest. Don't settle for less than a Lord Lieutenant for yourself.

Sancho Panza An island would do nicely. I should not turn my nose up at it.

Don Quixote So it's a deal.

Sancho Panza It's a bargain.

He runs at speed back home to pack for the journey.

Quick, before he changes his mind: fardel, bandages, ointments and salves, figs, raisins, onion, cheese –

Teresa Panza Are you moving out?

Sancho Panza We're moving up

Teresa Panza You've found a job? That's wonderful. You've never had a proper job before.

Sancho Panza Kindly address your remarks in a manner befitting a future governor.

Teresa Panza No one ever gave a slob like you a job. Why should they start now?

Sancho Panza I shall be squire to Don Quixote, killing damsels and rescuing giants in distress.

Teresa Panza Don Quixote!

Sancho Panza You can tell she's impressed.

SCENE ELEVEN
THE ADVENTURE OF THE WINDMILLS

Don Quixote, Sancho Panza, Rosinante and Dapple, Sancho's ass.

Don Quixote Now, you have the fardel.

Sancho Panza The fardel, yes.

Don Quixote And what is that?

Sancho Panza My ass.

Don Quixote Your ass.

Sancho Panza This is Dapple, my ass. You didn't expect me to walk, did you?

Don Quixote Not in the least. It's just that, somehow, I've never read of squire being mounted on an ass. Still I am sure that we shall shortly vanquish some mounted foe, and I shall win you a more honourable beast. But, look! Sancho, fortune already smiles on us. Look! More than thirty monstrous giants. I shall fight with them and take all their lives, and we shall enrich ourselves with the spoils. For this is lawful war, and we shall be doing God a service, wiping these giants off the face of the earth.

Sancho Panza What giants?

Don Quixote Over there on the hillside, waving their long arms, a sight to chill the very marrow of the soul.

Sancho Panza Sir, those are not giants. Those are windmills.

Don Quixote Windmills?

Sancho Panza New-fangled things for grinding corn. And what look like arms, waving about in the wind, those are the sails that make the millstones go.

Don Quixote I can see you know nothing of adventures. You are still hobbled by the prosaic side of your nature. These are giants, Sancho Panza, and if you are afraid of them my strong advice to you is to step aside and start saying your prayers while I engage them in a fierce unequal combat. Go for them now, Rosinante.

At the sound of his name, Rosinante rears up. Don Quixote advances.

Fly not, you cowards and vile caitiffs. A single knight fearlessly challenges you, regardless of the odds.

A wind begins to rise, and we see the windmills.

Assist me now, Dulcinea!

Don Quixote points his lance at the first windmill and charges. The lance gets caught in the sail, and Don Quixote is lifted in the air and whirled around, before being dumped back on earth.

Sancho Panza God save me. God save us all. Didn't I warn you to watch out? These are windmills.

Don Quixote Peace, peace, Sancho Panza. War is full of these tumbles, these reverses of fortune. And I am absolutely convinced that that wizard Friston, who stole my library and all the books in it, changed these giants into windmills, with the specific aim of depriving me of my glory. That's how deep it goes, his enmity. But let him do his worst – his wicked arts will be no match for my sword . . . My sword?

Sancho is putting him back together again. He finds the missing sword and helps him back on to Rosinante.

Sancho Panza Sir, can you sit upright, You seem to be riding half side-saddle. Probably because you were so bruised by the fall.

Don Quixote True. If you never hear me complain, that's because knights errant are not allowed to complain of any wound whatever, even if their entrails are tumbling out.

Sancho Panza You mean even if you're stuffing your guts back in with your own hands . . .

Don Quixote Mum's the word.

Sancho Panza Does the same thing apply to squires?

Don Quixote As far as I know, squires are at liberty to complain as much as they please.

Sancho Panza You mean, different rules apply.

Don Quixote Different rules apply.

Sancho Panza That's good.

Don Quixote For instance, even if you see me in the greatest peril in the world, you must not lay your hand on your sword to defend me – unless of course you see me attacked by a vile mob or some bunch of scoundrels. In that case you may assist me. But if there are other knights involved, it is in no wise lawful or allowed by the laws of chivalry. You must not intermeddle until you are dubbed a knight.

Sancho Panza I shall not intermeddle. You will find me most punctilious in this. I will observe this precept religiously.

SCENE TWELVE
THE FIGHT WITH THE BISCAYAN

A procession on the road. Two Benedictine Monks on mules, wearing travelling masks and carrying umbrellas. The Monks are attended by lackeys. Behind them a coach accompanied by men of horseback. In the coach, a lady accompanied by a lady's lady.

Benedictine Monk Music

Monks
Letabundus reedit
Avium concentur.
Ver jocundum prodiit,
Gaudeat iuventus.

Nova ferens gaudia
Modo vernant omnia.
Phoebus serenatur.
Redolens temperiem
Nava flore faciem
Flora renovatur.

Don Quixote Unless my eyes deceive me, this will prove the most famous adventure ever. For those black apparitions are undoubtedly enchanters.

Sancho Panza This could be worse than the windmills. Sir, those are Benedictine monks.

Don Quixote I have told you before, you know nothing about adventures.

He places himself in the road so as to block the progress of the travellers.

Diabolical and monstrous race, either release the highborn princess you are abducting in this coach, or prepare for instant death.

First Monk Señor Cavalier, we are neither diabolical nor monstrous. We are a couple of Benedictine monks minding our own business.

Don Quixote Soft words like soapsuds mean nothing to me. I know who you are. Assist me now, Dulcinea.

He spurs his horse and attacks with his lance at the ready, missing the first Monk by inches and causing him to slide off his mule. The second Monk flees. Sancho Panza rushes forward to take advantage of the Monk on the ground and strip him of his robe. Two lackeys come up. Don Quixote approaches the coach.

Lady, your haughty ravishers lie prostrate at your feet –

Lady My ravishers!

Don Quixote – overthrown by my invincible arm. I shall not keep you in suspense. Know then that I am called Don Quixote de La Mancha, knight errant and adventurer and captive in love to the beauteous Lady Dulcinea del Toboso. In return for the benefit you have received at my hands, all I require is for you to return to Toboso –

An immense bruiser, the Biscayan, comes up to the coach.

– and present yourself before that lady, and tell her what I have done to obtain your liberty.

The Biscayan takes hold of Don Quixote's lance.

Biscayan Be off with you. I swear by the God that made me, if you do not get out of the way of this coach, you'll be done for. I come from the Bay of Biscay. We're a stormy people. We're trouble, big trouble, and we say what we mean.

Don Quixote If you were a gentleman, which I see you are not, I would already have punished your presumption, you pitiable milksop.

Biscayan Throw down your lance and draw your sword and you will see how I can fight, you lying Manchego cheesemonger.

Don Quixote Cheesemonger? We shall see about that.

Sancho Panza That was below the belt – cheesemonger.

As Don Quixote advances, the Biscayan reaches into the coach for a cushion, which he uses as a shield. He is riding a mule, and is thus at a disadvantage. The two go at each other with astonishing ferocity.

Ladies Help. Help. Let the man go. Surely you can see he's mad.

Biscayan Stay out of it, you women, or I shall slice you in pieces.

He lands a hefty blow on Don Quixote's shoulders. Clang of metal against chainmail.

Don Quixote O lady of my soul, Dulcinea, flower of all beauty, this one's for you!

The Ladies get out of the coach, kneel down and begin to chant in terror. The fight continues.
The Biscayan raises his sword over Don Quixote's head.

Sancho Panza He's a dead man, my master. Now I shall never win my island.

Biscayan Cheesemonger, you die!

At a blow from the Biscayan, Don Quixote's helmet comes off.

Don Quixote That was my ear! Now taste the wrath of Don Quixote.

He lands a heavy blow on the Biscayan, whose mule throws him off. Don Quixote leaps from his horse and points his sword between the Biscayan's eyes.

Yield or I shall cut off your head.

Sancho Panza You're not serious.

Don Quixote It is my most solemn intention, here and now.

Sancho Panza You mean – in front of these ladies? Cut his head off?

Don Quixote Assuredly.

Sancho Panza faints. The Ladies scream. Don Quixote moves into position as if to carry out his threat.

Ladies Spare him. Spare him for our sakes.

Don Quixote Ladies, if you say so, I am bound to obey you. I shall spare him, but on one condition, which is that you return to Toboso and present this man to the peerless Dulcinea. She may dispose of him as she thinks fit.

Lady We will, we will. Let's get out of here.

They go.

Sancho Panza That was completely and utterly unexpected. We've won! We've won!

Don Quixote Ahem.

Sancho Panza You've won. And now I humbly request you, as you promised, to give me the government of that island which you have won.

Don Quixote Brother Sancho –

Sancho Panza (*aside*) Brother, he calls me brother.

Don Quixote Bandage! . . . This little adventure is not an adventure of islands, but a trivial affair of the crossroads. There's nothing to be gained from this sort of minor scrap –

Sancho Panza (*aside*) Minor scrap, he calls it. Did you hear that? What a man!

Don Quixote – beyond a broken head or the loss of an ear. But be patient. There will be more adventures soon, as a result of which I may make you not only the governor of an island, but something better.

Sancho Panza Something better, he says. Better than a governor would be a king. Better than a king would be, would be a god. Better than a god would be . . . What would be better than a god? Sancho Panza, the world lies at your feet.

SCENE THIRTEEN
A QUESTION OF FOOD

Don Quixote I wonder, Sancho Panza, if you have anything to eat in that fardel of yours. In a few moments we shall go in quest of a castle, so it might be a good idea to eat first.

Sancho Panza I have here an onion and a piece of cheese and some crusts of bread, but unfortunately I have nothing fit for so valiant a knight as your worship.

Don Quixote I don't think you understand. It is a matter of honour for knights errant not to eat more than once a month in the course of their quests. But when they do eat, it must be whatever comes to hand – that piece of cheese, for instance – no, *that* one – is exactly the sort of *haphazard provender* that knights errant subsist on. And – bread, please. I'll take a slice of that onion. From time to time, in some richly appointed castle, you – is that a fig there? – will find them entertained to some sumptuous banquet – *but* – and it is a big but – for the most part their most usual diet consisted of exactly the sort of rustic viands that you now offer me.

Sancho Panza Pardon me, sir. As I told you before, I can neither read nor write, so you wouldn't expect me to be well acquainted with the rules of the profession. From now on I shall bring a supply of dried fruits and berries and onion for your worship,. And for myself I shall bring poultry.

Don Quixote I did not say, Sancho, that knights errant are obliged to eat nothing but dried fruit. Simply that their most usual diet was of that kind, along with certain herbs and roots they used to find in the fields.

Sancho Panza I'm delighted to hear of these herbs and roots. I'm inclined to think that one day we will have occasion to make use of that knowledge. Acorn?

Don Quixote Acorn! Thank you. Mmm. Interesting . . . Do you eat the cup or – no, I thought not. Men lived on acorns once, you know, and sheep's cheese. It was an age of gold.

The Age of Gold

Don Quixote
It was a golden age. No one thought to work the land.
It was a happy time.
The oak trees pressed their fruit into your hand.
And tap your shoulder with a bough
And say – as you did –

Sancho Panza When?

Don Quixote Just now:
'Care for an acorn, brother man?
Eat all the acorns that you can
A sheet of cork, to stop the cold?'
It was an age of gold.
There was, no 'mine' and 'thine'.
No sense of dress in days long gone
There were no clothes –

Sancho Panza No clothes!

Don Quixote
The shepherdesses scampered round with nothing on –

Sancho Panza
And I s'pose they'd fig leaves for the men?

Don Quixote
They had great use for fig leaves then –

Sancho Panza
> And when the leaves began to fall?
> Or if the leaves were rather small?

Don Quixote
> They'd grab a sheep when they got cold.
> It was an age of gold.

Sancho Panza
> Their homes were made of cork.
> They gorged themselves on nuts and fruits.

Don Quixote
> Not gorged. They had enough.
> And picked out simple shepherd tunes on lilac flutes.

Sancho Panza
> They shared their wives with other men?

Don Quixote
> They had no word for marriage then.
> At night they slept in one great bed.

Sancho Panza
> Well, there's no telling where that led!

Don Quixote
> They had to huddle 'gainst the cold.

Both
> It was the Age of Gold.

SCENE FOURTEEN
MARCELA AND CHRYSOSTOM

A group of Shepherds, dressed in mourning, comes through the forest. They bring a body for burial.

Don Quixote Friends, what are you doing, dressed all in black, your brows wreathed in cypress and rosemary?

Shepherd We have come to bury Chrysostom, our dear companion.

Don Quixote Here in unhallowed ground?

Shepherd It was his wish. He was a wise man and a scholar, but a sad love impelled him here to live and die –

Second Shepherd A sad and unrequited love.

Shepherd He loved Marcela, a cruel, arrogant and disdainful beauty.

Beauty is Cruel

Don Quixote
I thank the spiders by the looking-glass,
Weaving their webs all night.
So I don't have to see my features as I pass
And give myself a fright.

I know that, by most conventional reckonings
I'm somewhat advanced in years.
But still, I find my soul tormented by such things
(Such things as love, I mean)
And I'm not too old for tears.

Ah my Lady Dulcinea.

Beauty is cruel.
All the poets say so.
Beauty is heartless.
All the books agree.
Though you ignore me,
Though you turn away so,
You will always be
Beautiful to me.

What drives these women wild when they are young?
What makes these girls as angry as the sea?
Where do they find that rage? What sharpens their
    tongue?

They answer their mothers back. They terrify me.

Overnight they've become beautiful women with
   the power
To wound a man to the quick with a toss of the hair.
And suddenly they know their strength.
They smoulder and they glower.
They have found the will to hurt, and they don't care.

Second Shepherd That's her! See how she makes her way down the mountainside.

Shepherd Are you not satisfied, Marcela? Must you come here to see his wounds open afresh? Perched like a basilisk upon the rock above his grave.

Second Shepherd Beauty viewing the corpse, viewing her victim.

Marcela You do me wrong to blame me, and I have come here to vindicate myself. Heaven made me handsome, as you all have said. But a beautiful woman is not to be blamed for her beauty, just as the viper is not to be blamed for her sting, though she can kill with it. Her sting is something given her by nature.

Beauty in a modest woman is like a fire at a distance – it will not burn those who do not come near. I was born free, and I chose to live free. I chose the trees in the mountains to be my companions. I chose these rocks for my home, these streams for my looking-glass. I kept my beauty to myself. I was like a fire at a distance.

Chrysostom here, on this very spot where you are digging his grave, told me of his love. I told him that my plan was to live in perpetual solitude, that the earth alone should enjoy the spoils of my beauty. I never deceived him or gave him reason for hope. If I had, then – yes – I would be much to blame. But if a woman is loved, is she obliged to love in return? I think not. Heaven has not yet ordained that I should love by destiny; and from loving by choice, I desire to be excused.

Don Quixote Do not pursue her on pain of incurring my furious indignation. She has made her case and she should not be held to blame for the death of Chrysostom. She never countenanced the desires of any of her admirers. Far from it. Her intentions were always virtuous. She should be honoured for this, not persecuted.

> Love is a torment.
> Love's a little urchin
> All the authorities
> Warn us to beware.
> He has a bow and
> Yes, he has an arrow.
> To wound you
> Or trap you in his snare.

Every knight, Sancho, should have a sort of surname by which he is known throughout the world of chivalry. From now on I shall be known as the Knight of the Sorrowful Countenance.

Sancho Panza A name well chosen.

Don Quixote How so?

Sancho Panza You look like you haven't eaten for week and you keep losing your teeth. Do you want to hear a story?

SCENE FIFTEEN
DON QUIXOTE AND THE SHEEP

Don Quixote You see on the horizon over there, that great cloud of dust?

Sancho Panza It seems to be coming towards us.

Don Quixote This is my lucky day, Sancho. Today I shall perform such exploits as shall be written in the book of fame for all succeeding ages. That cloud of dust is raised by a prodigious army of innumerable nations, coming this way.

Sancho Panza There must be two armies. Look, over there. Another cloud.

Don Quixote You are right. Two great armies, and in a moment they will meet and engage in battle right here.

Sancho Panza Oh no, what are we to do?

Don Quixote We must go to the assistance of the weaker side.

Sancho Panza The *weaker* side?

Don Quixote The army over there is led by the great emperor Alifanfaron, Lord of the Island of Trapobana. The other army is that of his great enemy, Pentapolin, King of the Garamantes.

We become aware of a noise in the distance which, as it approaches, will turn out to be the bleating of two converging flocks of sheep.

The knight you see there in the gilded armour, bearing a shield with a lion crowned, couchant at a damsel's feet – that's Laurcalco, Lord of the Silver Bridge. But the other one –

Sancho Panza Wait a moment. I haven't –

Don Quixote The other one with the armour flowered with gold, who bears three crowns argent in a field azure, that is Micocolembo, Grand Duke of Quirocia. At his side, the gigantic Brandabarbaran of Boliche. Do you see the Duke of Nerbia?

Sancho Panza I think so. Yes! . . . No, which is he?

Don Quixote Do you not hear the rattle of the drums, the sound of the trumpets, the neighing of the steeds?

35

Sancho Panza I hear nothing but the bleating of sheep and lambs.

Don Quixote That is the effect of your fear. That is what fear does to a man. It affects the senses. You can no longer see things as they are. Well, if you are so afraid, stand aside and let me go it alone.

Two flocks of sheep converge on stage.

Sancho Panza Wait, Don Quixote. There are no knights or giants here. These are sheep. You are going off to fight sheep.

Don Quixote Ho, knights! You that follow and fight under the banner of the valiant Emperor Pentapolin of the Naked Arm, follow me all of you!

He attacks the sheep.

Shepherds Here, you! What the devil do you think you're doing? Lay off our sheep.

Don Quixote fights the sheep. The Shepherds try stoning him. Then they pile in and beat him up.

Is the mad guy dead? Yes. Let's get out of here. How many sheep did he kill? Looks like five. Let's go before anyone finds us.

Sancho Panza Didn't I tell you? Didn't I? That was a flock of sheep. And now you're dead

Silence from Don Quixote for a while. Sancho weeps.

Don Quixote It is strange, is it not, Sancho –

Sancho Panza It is strange, yes.

Don Quixote The depth of the malignity we encounter in the world. That enemy of mine, that wizard Friston, envious of the glory I was about to gain in battle, transformed these squadrons into flocks of sheep. But do something for me, Sancho. Just follow them over the brow of the hill and you will see them turn back into human form again.

You promised you would tell me a story. Tell it.

Sancho Panza Very well. In a village in Estremedura, there was a shepherd. Well, he was a goatherd. This shepherd or goatherd was called Lope Ruiz. And this Lope Ruiz was in love with a shepherdess called Torralva. And this shepherdess, this Torralva was daughter to a rich herdsman, and this herdsman –

Don Quixote If you tell your story like this, repeating everything twice, it'll take days. Stick to the point. Be concise.

Sancho Panza So this shepherd Lope Ruiz was in love with the shepherdess Torralva –

Don Quixote I think I'm going to die.

Sancho Panza – and she had this way of making Lope Ruiz jealous over all kinds of small things. And in the end she made him so jealous that he began to hate her so much that he would do anything to avoid the sight of her. He decided to up sticks and leave his native land, taking his goats with him.

Don Quixote So they *were* goats.

Sancho Panza But Torralva, as soon as she found herself disdained by Lope, decided she was in love with him after all.

Don Quixote This is indeed what women are like. They love where they are slighted, and slight where they are loved.

Sancho Panza So Lope gathered his goats together and went over the plains of Estremedura in order to cross into Portugal. Torralva got wind of this, and began to follow Lope. He came to the river Guadiana. There was no boat, no ferryman, and he could only find a fisherman with a boat so small – pay attention now – it could only hold one man and one goat. He had three hundred goats. So he persuaded the fisherman to take the goats over, one at a time.

The fisherman got into the boat and carried over one goat, came back and got another goat, came back, got another goat, came back and got another goat. Now, you have to keep track of the goats. He returned for another goat, and another and another.

Don Quixote Say he carried them all over. At this rate it's going to take months.

Sancho Panza How many goats have passed already?

Don Quixote How the devil should I know?

Sancho Panza Didn't I tell you to keep track of the goats? I can go no further.

Don Quixote You mean, you need the exact number of goats.

Sancho Panza That's what I told you. And when you said you did not know, the rest of the story escaped my memory. Which is a pity because it was an edifying story . . .

Don Quixote Wait. What is that? Something gleaming in the distance.

SCENE SIXTEEN
THE HELMET OF MAMBRINO

Don Quixote Halt, knight, and explain yourself.

Travelling Barber Your worship, you do me too much honour. I am not a knight, I am a travelling barber, working between two small villages.

Don Quixote A barber! and wearing a helmet of the purest gold? You expect me to believe that?

Barber A helmet? What can he mean? Oh, you mean my basin. Oh yes, yes, it must look odd. Yes, yes, deary me, I was caught in that rain a few moments ago, and, you see, I'm wearing a new hat, and I didn't want it ruined, so I put the old brass basin over the hat, like so, and forgot all about it. Good day to you, sir.

Don Quixote Halt and defend yourself, or surrender to me what is so justly my due.

Barber Surrender what? Hey, what is this?

Don Quixote attacks him with his lance. The Barber runs off in terror.

Don Quixote Pick up the helmet, Sancho.

Sancho Panza That's a nice basin. Worth a few bob.

Sancho gives Don Quixote the basin, which the Don Quixote puts on his head.

Don Quixote The pagan for whom this helmet was made must have had a prodigious large head. And alas there's a piece missing. What are you laughing at, Sancho?

Sancho Panza I'm laughing to think what a huge head the pagan had, who owned this helmet which, for all the world, looks just like a barber's basin.

Don Quixote You know, Sancho, in all the books I have read about chivalry, I never came across a squire who talked back to his master as much as you do.

Sancho Panza From now on I shall not open my mouth.

Don Quixote You know what I think, Sancho. I think this famous piece, Mambrino's helmet – look at the workmanship, just look at it – this enchanted helmet must, by some strange accident, have fallen into the hands of someone who, being ignorant of its true value, but realising it to be of pure gold, melted down one part of it and, with the other part made this, which – as you correctly point out, Sancho – does rather look like a barber's bowl. I shall have it restored, of course. But for the moment I shall wear it as it is. Something is better than nothing, Sancho. Something is better than nothing.

Sancho Panza Sir, may I speak?

Don Quixote Of course.

Sancho Panza Would it not be better instead of wandering through these waste places with nobody to see our brave deeds – just to find some great prince who is fighting a war and enter his service?

Don Quixote That may seem a good point to you, Sancho, but the thing is, this wandering around the world is a form of probation. You have to notch up some deeds of fame and renown, Then when you show yourself at the gates of a great city, your fame has gone ahead of you. All the boys come out and follow you, shouting: 'It is the Knight of the Sun! It is the Knight of the Serpent!' The thrill is palpable The ladies gaze modestly down from their high balconies.

SCENE SEVENTEEN
DON QUIXOTE AND THE CHAIN GANG

Oh Run to the Door

Galley Slaves
Oh run, run to the door, oh run, run to the door,
Oh run, run to the door . . . oh run, run to the door.

Oh run to the door, Mother, run to the door
And look in the eyes of your son

And bid me farewell as they take me away
　　Forgive me for what I have done
And watch till I come to the dip in the road
　　Forgive me for what I have done.

Oh come from the fell, brother, come from the fell
　　And fetch down the flock from the fold
And comfort your mother and weep with her now
　　And weep where your father lies cold
And watch with her now through the heat of the night
　　And weep where your father lies cold.

They have taken the vinegar sponge to his head.
　　And wrung out his blood in a bowl.
Let them wash all the hatred from out of his heart.
　　And rinse out the bile from his soul.
Let them wash all the vengefulness out of his heart
　　The bitterness out of his soul.

There's a ship in the bay where the winds are at play.
　　A bench that is waiting for me.
And the law of the ship is the chain and the whip,
　　The chain and the whip and the sea.
I am bound by the law to the chain and the whip.
　　I'm bound by a chain to the sea.

Oh run to the door, Mother, run to the door
　　And look in the eyes of your son.
I am dead. I am dead as the father I killed.
　　Forgive me for what I have done.
I am chained. I am led to the Ship of the Dead.
　　Oh Mother, forgive your dead son.
Oh Mother, forgive your dead son.

Chain-gang appears, with Guards.

Sancho Panza It's a chain of galley slaves, poor souls
forced by the King to the galleys, strung out like a row of
beads.

Don Quixote How can that be? Is it possible the King would force anyone?

Sancho Panza I'm not saying he does or he doesn't.

Don Quixote Gentlemen of the guard, tell me why you are conducting these wretches in this manner.

Guard These are His Majesty's slaves, on the way to the galley. That's all I know about the matter. If you want to know how they got into this evil plight, ask them yourself.

Don Quixote You, friend, what brings you here?

Galley Slave I fell in love.

Don Quixote In that case I should be rowing alongside you, if falling in love is a crime.

Galley Slave I fell in love with a basket of fine linen, and I embraced it so close they had to prise it from my hands. Well, I was lucky to be caught in the act, so I was spared torture. They gave me a hundred lashes and have sent me, as a special bonus, for three years on the galleys.

Don Quixote Why that man, why does he wear more shackles than the rest?

Guard That is Gines de Pasamonte, a famous villain. He's going down for ten years which is a sort of civil death. He has written his own life.

Don Quixote Does he write well?

Gines As well as heart could wish.

Don Quixote What is the title of your book?

Gines *The Life of Gines de Pasamonte.*

Don Quixote And is it finished?

Gines How can it be finished? My life is not yet finished. But what I have to say, I already have by heart.

Don Quixote Why does your friend hang his head so low?

Galley Slave This gentleman is what we call a canary bird, a musician and a singer.

Don Quixote Must men be punished for singing?

Galley Slave Sing once, and weep your life away.

Don Quixote I don't understand.

Guard In their slang, to sing in agony is to confess upon the rack. That man was put to torture and confessed to being a cattle thief. That got him six years and two hundred lashes.

Second Guard The men who sing are the scum of the galley. Their fellows despise them for not having the courage to say no. Say yes and you betray yourself. Betray yourself and you betray all of them. That's what they think.

Don Quixote I think so too. My dear friends, my unfortunate brothers, I have seen and heard enough to know that you go to the galleys much against the grain. And it seems true that your cases did not always come off as in justice they ought to have done. I will entreat these gentlemen, your guards, to let you go in peace. There is a God in heaven –
  To punish the wicked and reward the good.

Guard Oh yes, very funny.

Don Quixote Why should an honest man punish another, when he himself has no interest in the matter? These men have not wronged you. And so I calmly and gently request you to let them go. Otherwise this sword, this lance and the strength of my arm will be obliged to force you.

Guard You want us to let the King's prisoners go, as if we had the authority to set them free. Be on your way with your basin on your head.

Sancho Panza Be careful, sir. Justice – that is the King himself – he only punishes them for their crimes.

Don Quixote attacks the Guard unexpectedly with his lance.

Don Quixote You are a cat and a rat and a rascal to boot.

Guard Well I'll be . . .

Before the other Guards have realised what is happening, the Galley Slaves break their chains and overwhelm them.

Don Quixote Go now in gratitude all of you to the noble city of Toboso and –

Galley Slave That one-horse shit-hole!

Don Quixote Why then, you son of a whore, if you've no gratitude . . .

The Galley Slaves begin pelting Don Quixote and Sancho Panza with rocks. They steal some of their things before escaping.

SCENE EIGHTEEN
THE MADNESS OF DON QUIXOTE

Sancho Panza Why are we wandering through these remote and rocky places, far from any human habitation?

Don Quixote Haven't I told you? I plan to imitate the knights of the old romances in this: they often went mad. Orlando, for instance, when he thought his loved one had been unfaithful to him, went mad for grief. He tore up trees, killed shepherds, massacred sheep, set fire to cottages –

Sancho Panza Yes, but –

Don Quixote – demolished houses, rampaged through rivers, dragged mares to the ground –

Sancho Panza Yes, but –

Don Quixote – and did a hundred thousand other things, worthy to be recorded, and which indeed he is remembered for. You said 'Yes, but –'

Sancho Panza It seems to me that the knights who acted in this manner were provoked to it. Orlando had reason to believe that his girl was playing fast and loose with a rival. What's Dulcinea done to make you think she's having it off with anyone?

Don Quixote That's the whole point. That's the beauty of my plan. A knight who goes mad with just cause deserves no thanks. But to do so without reason is the business. To go mad without reason is to say to my lady – to let her understand what I should perform in the wet, if this is what I do in the dry.

Sancho Panza What you should perform in the wet?

Don Quixote I shall give you this letter to take to the Lady Dulcinea. You must tell her I have gone mad. If her answer is kind and encouraging, I shall stop being mad. But if I don't get the answer my fidelity deserves, I shall go really, really mad. And then she'll be sorry. In short, mad I am and mad I must be until you return with her reply. Now, you haven't yet seen me mad. So, before you go, I'd like you to see me – well, I insist that you see me – cavorting naked –

Sancho Panza Oh no, please.

Don Quixote Just a dozen or two mad pranks. It'll only take half an hour.

Sancho Panza Oh no, sir, please, not naked. Please. I couldn't bear it. Sir. Oh my Lord, he's taking his clothes off.

The Priest and the Barber are watching from the distance. They have a cart with a cage.

Priest There they are. And it looks as if we've just arrived in the nick of time.

Now for our intervention. Here. Put on this dress.

Barber Wait a moment. I thought you were going to dress up as Dulcinea.

Priest It is beneath the dignity of priesthood.

Barber What about my dignity? and what about my beard?

Priest Take this as a veil. He's stripping to his undershirt.

Barber (*in a woman's voice*) Where is the valorous Don Quixote de La Mancha, the only object of my heart's affections?

Don Quixote Who calls my name?

Barber I, Dulcinea del Toboso. I call your name, Don Quixote. I call your name. Come to my carriage. Come to be comforted.

Don Quixote Hunger, thirst and the heat have done their work. I hear the voice of Lady Dulcinea. Yet what I see reminds me of someone else.

Barber Come now to the bosom that pants for you.

Sancho Panza What panting bosom is this?

Barber We've come to take him home, Sancho, it's for his own good. Help us before it's too late.

Priest comes up behind Don Quixote, carrying an enormous butterfly net or keep-net.

Don Quixote Treachery. Help me, Sancho.

Priest Got him. Now get him into the cage.

Sancho Panza Master, I must not intermeddle.

SCENE NINETEEN
THE HOMECOMING

Back in the village.

Boy They're back, they're back and they've put him in a cage.

Niece What's going on?

Boy The priest and the barber have put my master in a cage.

Niece They can't do that. Where are they?

She goes off with the Boy to look for them. Enter Sancho and Teresa.

Teresa Panza So you're back, husband. Did you bring me home a petticoat? Did you bring shoes for your children?

Sancho Panza I bring other things of greater consequence.

Teresa Panza Perhaps you would like to show me these things. They might do my heart some good. You've been gone a long time, and I've had to fend for myself as best I could.

Sancho Panza I'll tell you when we get home.

Teresa Panza Tell me now or we may not 'get home'.

Sancho Panza Keep your voice down. The agreement is that in the *second* half of our adventures . . .

Teresa Panza Second half! Second half!

Sancho Panza I have cast-iron guarantees that I shall become either an earl or a governor of an island. And not just any old island either, but one of the very best to be had.

Teresa Panza What's all this talk about islands? I don't understand.

Sancho Panza You'll see. You'll be amazed. I'll tell you something though. For an honest man there's nothing to beat the life of a squire to a knight errant. It's true that most adventures don't end up exactly as you might wish. But for all that it's a fine thing to go looking for the unexpected: crossing mountains, exploring woods, climbing rocks, visiting castles and inns, and the devil a farthing to pay.

Oh dear, here he comes.

Don Quixote is brought in in a cage.

The Devil a Farthing to Pay

Sancho Panza
To give up your hearth and your home
For the life of a knight and a squire –
It's the highest a hope can attain.
Its the highest a man can aspire.
When you live for the thrill of the hour
When you thrill to the gift of the day
And the Devil a farthing to pay.

Teresa Panza
But what is a women do to
When her husband goes off with some man
And she's left with a house full of kids
To fend for herself as she can?
And she's borrowed until she's ashamed
And her neighbours are all the same way
For we're all up to here with our debts
And the devil a farthing to pay.

Don Quixote
Though I find myself stuck in a cage
When it comes to a push or a shove
Every soul has a right to its rage.
Every heart has a right to its love.

Every bird has a right to its nest.
Every dog has a right to its day.
Every knight has a right to his quest
And the devil a farthing to pay.

Chorus

    The devil a penny
    The devil a groat
The devil a sixpence to keep you afloat
    The devil a dollar
    The devil a pound
The devil a shilling to buy the next round.

Though the world is a cell or a cage
When it comes to a push or a shove
Every soul has a right to its rage.
Every heart has a right to its love.
Every bird has a right to its nest.
Every dog has a right to its day.
Every knight has a right to his quest
And the devil a farthing to pay!
And the devil a farthing to pay!

Act Two

SCENE ONE
DON QUIXOTE ASLEEP

Don Quixote is in bed asleep. The Niece and the Housekeeper have been looking after him by turns.

Wake Now

Niece
 Where are you riding to? O troubled soul,
  I heard you call in your sleep.
 I saw you strike out at some pestering foe.
  Some hand was dragging you,
 Some hand was dragging you down to the deep.

Don Quixote Three giants . . . again . . . have at you . . .

Niece Still the same story, the endless duelling.

Housekeeper It doesn't seem to improve.

 Was it a river bank? Was it a shore?
  You seemed to halt in your quest
 And I was afraid to shake you awake before
  You had fought off that hand
 You had fought off that hand and come into your rest.

 I see you have won it now. I was afraid.
  They say men meet death in their dreams
 And they must be left on their own with that shade,
  Fight on that lonely shore
 Fight by those streams.

Don Quixote Caraculiambro, you die!

 I see you stirring, I see you ride back
  Home like a soldier on leave

Bringing a bargain from Death in your pack
    Were life nothing more
Were life nothing more than a scribbled reprieve.

Wake now to a welcome reprieve.
    Wake now to a welcome reprieve.

The Priest and the Barber approach the house of Don Quixote, speaking in whispers.

Barber So whatever you do don't mention – you know what.

Priest You mean knight-errantry.

Barber Shhh. I said whatever you do.

Priest Yes but –

Housekeeper Who's there?

Barber Me: Master Nicholas, the barber-surgeon, and the priest, Señor Pero Perez.

Priest How is he?

Niece He's fine, but will you please not mention you know what.

Priest You mean knight-errantry.

Voice of Don Quixote Do I hear voices? Are those my old friends? Come in. Come in.

Don Quixote is discovered sitting up in bed wearing a waistcoat of green baize and a red Toledo bonnet.

Barber Why, my dear friend, you look shrivelled up like a mummy.

Don Quixote I feel quite starved for news. What's been going on in the great world, while I've been lying here?

Barber Well, you know, we've all been getting on with our lives, quietly. It's been very quiet . . . That's just about it, really – a few chins to shave, hair to be cut, teeth pulled . . . a little minor surgery here and there, a little blood-letting, nothing to be alarmed about . . . nothing really.

Brief silence.

Priest You charmed a wart.

Barber Oh yes, that's true, but I don't suppose Don Quixote wants to hear about warts dropping off old ladies' noses.

Noises off.

SCENE TWO
THE RETURN OF SANCHO

The Niece and the Housekeeper are in the yard, trying to keep Sancho Panza from entering.

Housekeeper Go back to where you came from.

Sancho Panza Hey, what is this?

Niece Oh no you don't!

Don Quixote What in heaven's name is going on?

Housekeeper You're the one to blame. It was you seduced our master and led him astray.

Sancho Panza Excuse me, Mistress Housekeeper for the Devil. He's the one who seduced me; promising me an island, which by the way I'm still waiting for.

Niece Promised you an island, did he? What'll you do with an island then?

Sancho Panza What would I do with an island? I'd govern it! I'd govern, govern, govern!

Housekeeper What about going home and governing there for a change? What about setting your hand to the plough and trying to govern that for the first time in your life, Governor?

Don Quixote (*from his room*) Is that my squire, Sancho Panza? Will you women kindly stop screaming and let him come in? And my dear friends, if you would just leave us a moment, I have some business with this good man.

The Priest and the Barber leave Don Quixote with Sancho Panza.

Sancho Panza 'Good man' you are pleased to call me. And yet your household is instructed to humiliate and insult me.

Don Quixote I gave no such instructions, and most sincerely apologise for any insult you have received. But tell me, Sancho, what do folks say about me in town? What do you, the common people, think, and the gentlemen, the cavaliers?

Sancho Panza I shall tell you, on condition that you will not be angry. The common people take you for a downright madman, and me for no less of a fool. The gentlemen say that you have invaded the dignity of knighthood with nothing more than a paltry vineyard and a couple of acres of land and, as they put it, a tatter behind and a tatter before.

Don Quixote You see, Sancho, virtue is always persecuted.

Sancho Panza If you really want to get to the bottom of what people say about you, I shall introduce you to Samson Carrasco, who has just come back from studying in Salamanca. He tells me – you won't believe this – that your story is already printed in a book under the title *The Ingenious Gentleman, Don Quixote de La Mancha* –

you, the Lady Dulcinea and me Sancho Panza by name. Indeed, he told me several things that had passed between us when we were alone, so much that I crossed myself in amazement.

Don Quixote Depend on it, the author of this history must be some wizard or enchanter. Nothing is hidden from them when they have a mind to write.

Sancho Panza Samson Carrasco says the author's name is Cid Hamet Ben Engeli.

Don Quixote Cid Hamet Ben Engeli! A Moorish name.

Sancho Panza Jelly is very Moorish.

Don Quixote Bring Samson Carrasco without further ado.

Exit Sancho.

A wizard on my tail! a man of power following me wherever I go, waiting to pounce, waiting to frustrate me in my greatest adventures, turning giants into windmills and soldiers into sheep, and then – this is the strangest part – writing it all down and publishing it, as if to mock me. Well, I suppose I should take it as a compliment. My enemies must fear my grand design. But still, it rather shakes me. It reminds me that I am always, always being watched.

SCENE THREE
ENTER A WAG

Samson Carrasco Señor Don Quixote de La Mancha, let me have the honour of kissing your grandeur's hand. Your worship is one of the most famous knights errant –

Don Quixote Oof, I wouldn't say that. I wouldn't go quite so far. Go on.

Samson Carrasco – one of the most famous knights errant that have been, or shall be, upon the whole circumference of the earth. A blessing light upon Cid Hamet Ben Engeli, who has given us a history of your mighty deeds, and blessings upon blessings light upon that virtuoso, Miguel de Cervantes Saavedra, who went to the trouble to have them translated out of the Arabic and into our vulgar Castilian tongue.

Don Quixote So it is true that my story has been written, and that the man who composed it was a Moor and a sage.

Samson Carrasco My understanding is they have already shifted over twelve thousand copies in Valencia, Barcelona and Portugal. There's a rumour it's printing in Antwerp.

Don Quixote It is one of the things that should give the highest satisfaction to a virtuous and eminent man, to find his good name published and in print.

Samson Carrasco They have taken care to paint the gallant deportment of your worship to the life. The sage has left nothing at the bottom of the inkhorn, including the various drubbings you have both received.

Don Quixote *and* **Sancho Panza** Drubbings?

Don Quixote Well, it is true that we have had our ups and downs, but the sage might have had the delicacy to omit the downs. They don't alter the essential truth of a story, and sometimes, alas, they redound to the discredit of the hero.

Samson Carrasco But it is one thing to compose as a poet, and another to write as an historian.

Don Quixote You are correct. History is a sacred kind of writing, because truth is essential to it, and where truth is, there God himself is. But to talk wittily, and write amusingly are talents of a great genius only.

I suppose my history will need a commentary to make it intelligible.

Samson Carrasco Not at all, There is no difficulty in it. Children thumb it, boys read it, men understand it and old folks recommend it. In every nobleman's antechamber you can guarantee to find a group of pages sniggering over a copy.

Don Quixote *and* **Sancho Panza** Sniggering?

Samson Carrasco Sniggering . . . appreciatively over some of the more rough-and-tumble passages.

Don Quixote Señor Carrasco, I find all this rather much to take in at once. But I beg you to feel free to visit again, as often as you please.

Samson Carrasco Sire, you do me a great honour.

Exit Samson.

Don Quixote Pack that fardel of yours, Sancho, and saddle the admirable Dapple. We are off to Toboso. I shall confront the lady Dulcinea, and find out what she thought of that letter you delivered for me.

Sancho Panza Ah! The letter . . .

Don Quixote Toboso, my destiny!

Sancho Panza Pack me a fardel! Toboso my destiny. What a wonderful thing it must be to speak like that, on a grand impulse. The problem is, this letter, I never delivered it. But even if I had the letter still, whose hands should I entrust it to in Toboso? In Toboso! At the palace of the Lady Dulcinea? Dulcinea is a dream. These palaces are figments of my master's imagination.

THE PARLIAMENT OF DEATH

A fearsome company of Actors, performing in the Festival of Corpus Christi, travelling through the countryside. They come on a cart. They are dressed as Death, the Emperor, the Queen, the Soldier, the Devil, etc. They dance. The Devil sings the verses. There is an acrobat dressed as a skeleton.

Death the Acrobat

Actors
The King went off to his cloister.
He hid himself away
Where the bronze tombs of his ancestors
Were colder than the coldest clay
And he looked at the lovely crucifix
Hanging above his head
And a marble voice from a marble mouth
Spoke to the King and said:

Death sang a song to Solomon
Upon a broken lute
And Death for the Queen of Egypt
Came coiled in a basket of fruit
Death jumps with the juggler
And tumbles with the crew.
Death, Death the acrobat
Is coming to dance with you.

At the court of the Grand Inquisitor
The walls were hung with black
And they took the quaking heretic
And they stretched him on the rack
And they stepped aside for the torturer
And they turned from his face in fear

57

For they heard the words he whispered
In the Grand Inquisitor's ear:

Death sang a song to Solomon
Upon a broken lute
And Death for the Queen of Egypt
Came coiled in a basket of fruit.
Death jumps with the juggler
And tumbles with the crew.
Death, Death the acrobat
Is coming to dance with you.

And this boy plays the Angel
And this woman plays the Queen
And this man plays the Emperor
As fine as you've ever seen
And me – I play the Devil
And I know everything
For I dance in the Parliament of Death
And this is what I sing:

Death sang a song to Solomon
Upon a broken lute
And Death for the Queen of Egypt
Came coiled in a basket of fruit.
Death jumps with the juggler
And tumbles with the crew.
Death, Death the Acrobat
Is coming to dance
Is coming to dance
Is coming to dance with you!
BOOOOH!

In the course of this performance, Don Quixote and
Sancho Panza, with Rosinante and Dapple, have
entered.

Don Quixote Carter, coachman or Devil, tell me who
you are and where you are going.

Devil We are strolling players performing for Corpus Christi.

Don Quixote When first I saw you, I thought this was the beginning of some great adventure. But I see I was deceived. Go act your play and God be with you

One of the company, dressed in bells and with bladders on a stick, beats the ground around Rosinante, who panics. Sancho goes to help Don Quixote. The bladder-dancer jumps on Dapple and makes off with him.

Sancho Panza Why, that devil has run away with Dapple.

Don Quixote I will find him, though he hide in the deepest dungeons of hell.

Sancho Panza Sir, take my advice. Never meddle with actors. They are a people mightily beloved. I have seen an actor arrested for two murders get off scot-free. Everybody favours them, protects and assists them. They work for princes and they dress like princes. I'll find Dapple in the end.

Don Quixote No, I won't give that Devil a cause to brag. Hold, sirs! Let me teach you how to treat the asses of the squires of knights errant!

The Actors immediately form a defensive line around the cart, and prepare to throw rocks at Don Quixote.

Sancho Panza Sir, sir, remember, though these appear to be princes and emperors, there's not one genuine knight errant among them. They're just actors.

Don Quixote You are quite right. I neither can nor ought to draw my sword against any who are not dubbed knights. It's your task, Sancho. I will encourage and instruct you from the sidelines.

Sancho Panza There is no need to be revenged on anybody, sir. Good Christians do not demand revenge.

Don Quixote Then let us leave these phantoms.

SCENE FIVE
VISITING TOBOSO

Toboso by night.

Don Quixote Toboso the Fair, the legendary city –

Sancho Panza Watch where you step . . . oh no.

Don Quixote   – lit only by the moon and the stars. Sancho, lead on to the palace of Dulcinea. Maybe we shall find her awake in some small apartment of her castle . . .

Sancho Panza And bang on the door until she lets us in, like a couple of gallants at the gate of a bawdy house? Never taking no for an answer. At this time of night.

Don Quixote First let us find her castle. Lead on, I say.

Sancho Panza These Tobosans are a fierce lot, and proud of their honour. They won't like to find a couple of strangers inquiring after their women. Wait here and I'll go looking for the palace of Lady Dulcinea.

Don Quixote takes up his contemplative position, as Knight of the Sorrowful Countenance, leaning on his lance. Sancho addresses the audience.

Sancho Panza The truth is that this master of mine is mad enough to be tied to his bed. And the other truth is that I'm not far behind him – no, I'm madder than him, to follow and serve him and go on all these crazy errands for him. Still, if it keeps him happy, I'll see what I can make him believe.

Sir, come this way and you will behold the Princess Dulcinea. See how she's clad in cloth of gold, with strings of pearls and diamonds, her hair loose about her shoulders, like so many sunbeams. The mistress of your thoughts.

He kneels in front of first Peasant Woman.

Queen, princess and duchess of beauty, your captive knight stands yonder, paralysed in your presence. Be pleased to receive us kindly. I am Sancho Panza his squire, and he is the Knight of the Sorrowful Countenance, Don Quixote de La Mancha.

Don Quixote also kneels.

Peasant Woman Get out of the way and go hang yourself. I'm in a hurry.

Sancho Panza Princess of Toboso, doesn't your heart relent, to see the pillar and prop of knight-errantry kneeling before you here?

Peasant Woman Look at the way you minor gentry come and make fun of us poor country girls, as if we didn't know how to give as good as we get. You just go your way and let me go on mine. Goodbye.

Don Quixote Sancho, you see now the power of the enchantment under which I suffer – the power of these wizards, my enemies. You told me, and I must believe you, that I was in the presence of the Lady Dulcinea. Yet what I saw was a poor country wench.

Dulcinea has been transformed and I am determined to fight with every fibre of my being to return her to her true state and to her beauty.

SCENE SIX
THE KNIGHT OF THE MIRRORS

Samson Carrasco comes through the forest dressed as a knight errant, and in search of Don Quixote and Sancho Panza. He sees them before they are aware of him.

Samson Carrasco Who would have thought that a man could do such a thing – to read a book and then to step into the sequel? Yet I have already taken that step. I intervened, when I told the knight and his squire about their fame in the great world. And now that I have taken my first tentative steps into the river of the story, I intend to have a little fun. (*Groans.*) Aargh!

Sancho Panza What was that?

Don Quixote What was what?

Sancho Panza A voice.

Don Quixote What voice? A voice like a wizard?

Sancho Panza Like a wizard, yes. Are these woods full of wizards?

Don Quixote Crammed with wizards, yes. You can hardly move without stepping on a wizard.

Samson Carrasco Aaaah!

Don Quixote A wizard in pain?

Samson Carrasco Aaah. Woe is me. Woe is me.

Don Quixote An afflicted soul.

Samson Carrasco Afflicted indeed. I serve the most beautiful and ungrateful woman in the world – Casildea de Vandalia.

Don Quixote Casildea de Vandalia! The most ungrateful, I can believe, but the most beautiful, no!

Samson Carrasco The most consummately beautiful – I have caused her to be so acknowledged wherever I have wandered in the world. The noble knights of Navarre, the knights of Leon, the Andalusians to a man, and – mark my words – the knights of La Mancha to boot. What makes me proudest of all – between you and me, in all confidence – is that the famous Don Quixote de La Mancha was forced, by this my right hand, in single combat, lasting from dawn to dusk – was finally forced to acknowledge that my Casildea de Vandalia outshone in beauty his wretched Dulcinea del Toboso. Now this Don Quixote –

Sancho Panza This is outrageous, this is.

Don Quixote Hold your tongue, Sancho.

Sancho Panza I wouldn't put up with it. I mean, there are limits.

Don Quixote I said hold your tongue.

Samson Carrasco This Don Quixote had many noble exploits to his name. But at the end of a long, hard-fought day, when he lay sobbing at my feet and begging for mercy, when he admitted that Dulcinea was no better than she ought to be, really no more than a common village strumpet with a long history in the haystack – when he yielded every point to me, then all the glory of Don Quixote's exploits was transferred to my account. That's the way it works in knight-errantry. It's winner takes all.

Don Quixote Sancho, help me to my steed.

Sancho Panza I'd watch out if I were you, young man. I've never seen him like this.

Don Quixote My lance, Sancho. Stranger knight, I do not know whether to call you out as a liar, or to pity you as an honest man deceived by wizards and hobgoblins. Either way, since you persist in your claims, we must fight. I am Don Quixote de La Mancha, and I serve the Lady Dulcinea. Take up your lance.

Samson Carrasco My lance, yes, by all means.

Samson is not taking this entirely seriously.

Don Quixote Have at you.

Samson is unprepared and unseated.

Samson Carrasco Hey, that hurt. You surprised me.

Don Quixote Young man, you seem ill suited to the life of chivalry. I shall spare you today, for killing such a fool would not redound to my honour. But if I hear of your boastful lies again, I shall show no mercy. Come, Sancho.

Exit Don Quixote and Sancho Panza.

Samson Carrasco I miscalculated badly. All I wanted was to bring him home safely. It's what everyone in the village seems to want. I was only trying to help and have a little fun along the way. But what began as a joke has become an insult to my person. An insult to my person can only be remedied by revenge. We shall meet again, Don Quixote.

Sancho Panza The noble knights of Navarre! The knights of Leon! The Andalusians to a man indeed! And God only knows who that fool fought, who called himself Don Quixote!

And the things he said about Dulcinea. A long history in the haystack indeed! Well, he's not so boastful now, is he? Not now he's met the real Don Quixote. Soon put that pretender in his place, eh? Vanity is soon lost face down in the dirt. Pride goes before a – Sir, a lion!

SCENE SEVEN
THE KNIGHT AND THE LIONS

Don Quixote Don't mock me. I know your tricks. Lions indeed. Pah! When did you ever see a lion in La Mancha? The odd lynx, yes, I grant you. Lions, no sir.

A cart carrying two lions in cages has drawn up behind Don Quixote. The female lion reaches a paw through the bars of her cage and idly places it on Don Quixote's shoulder. Don Quixote distractedly brushes the paw off, without realising what it is. The lion replaces the paw on the shoulder. Don Quixote looks down and sees the paw.

Don Quixote Aha!

Lion-Keeper Don't move. You may frighten him.

Don Quixote I should hope I do frighten him. (*Deftly moving out of range.*) Who are you, sir, and where are you going with this savage cargo?

Lion-Keeper I work for the Governor of Oran, who is sending this large animal as a gift to the King. He's big and he's hungry (the lion, not the king), and we must get along and feed him.

Don Quixote Open his cage.

Sancho Panza Don't listen to him. I beg you. Pay no attention.

Lion-Keeper He's not serious, is he?

Sancho Panza No. He's . . .

Lion-Keeper Mad, is he?

Sancho Panza It's not mad exactly. It's –

Don Quixote Master Lion-Keeper, whichever wizards or enchanters sent you here, I shall let them know, beyond any doubt, that I am not the man to be scared by lions. As it stands, this lion is an affront to my valour, and that I cannot tolerate. Now, open the cage this instant or I shall take this sword and pin you to the cart.

Lion-Keeper One moment, sir. (*To Sancho.*) I would get out of the way if I were you, my friend.

Don Quixote Sancho, I shall fight this beast on foot. Now come forth, lion . . .

Lion-Keeper I'd commend your soul to God if I were you. This is going to be swift and bloody.

The cage door is opened. The lion gets up, stretches, yawns and turns around. It ignores Don Quixote.

Don Quixote Master keeper, can you just hit that lion for me. Do something to provoke it.

Lion-Keeper I cannot, sir. If I provoke the lion, I'll be the first to be eaten. You can't ask for that. Be satisfied, sir, don't tempt your luck a second time. You have proved your courage. You gave the lion a choice I'd say you won this hands down.

Don Quixote You think so? Honestly? Then shut the cage again, my good man. Sancho! Come down out of that tree. I am the Knight of the Lions, now.

Sancho Panza You can do that, can you?

Don Quixote Do what?

Sancho Panza Change your name at the drop of a hat.

Don Quixote I follow the ancient practice of knights errant who changed their names whenever it served their turn.

Sancho Panza Sometimes I think it would be better for me, much better, to return to my own house, to my wife and children, to maintain and bring them up with the little God is pleased to give me – to live simply at home instead of following Your Worship along roads that have long since petered out with dreadful food and nothing decent to drink, sleeping on bare earth, being chased by lions –

Don Quixote If you are so keen to go back to your wife and children – do so by all means. God forbid I should hinder you. You're the one looking after the money. Work out how long we've been on the road this time, decide how much you ought to be paid a month, and pay yourself. Go on. Pay yourself off.

Sancho Panza When I worked for Thomas Carrasco, Samson's father, I got two ducats a month plus board and lodging. It's hard work being a servant to a farmer but, however bad it may be, at the end of the day we got supper from the pot and we slept in a bed. With you, I sleep on hard ground in the open air in all kinds of weather, living on scraps of cheese, drinking from the streams –

Don Quixote You are right. Everything you say is true. How much do you think I should pay you more that Thomas Carrasco?

Sancho Panza There's the extra for my work. Then there's the promise you made me of the governorship of an island – I should get compensation for that.

Don Quixote And how do you calculate that?

Sancho Panza We must compute it from the day you promised me, to the present hour.

Don Quixote And that is?

Sancho Panza About twenty years and three days, more or less.

Don Quixote You mean about two months at most. I see you've decided you deserve all the money you are holding for me. Take it. Take it all. I hadn't realised quite what a scoundrel you are. Take everything and go.

Sancho Panza Sir . . . no, forgive me.

The Night Comes Down like a Cloak

The night comes down like a cloak.
The light is gone in the West.
The sheep are still in the fold.
My love lies asleep on my breast.
Sleep on, my love, sleep on.
Your child wakes in my womb.
Come sunrise you'll be gone.

Oh he loved me more in the dark
Than ever he did in the day.
I dare not stir for the fear
When he wakes he will up and away.
Sleep on, my love, sleep on.
Your child wakes in my womb.
Come sunrise you'll be gone.

  For love belongs to the night
  As the wolf belongs to the hill.
  A man may move in the dark
  As a fox moves in for the kill.

  A kiss can stifle a cry.
  A mouth can smother a breath.
  Love can ruin a life.
  Love makes a gift of a death.

  And love can ruin a life
  As a crop can ruin a tree.

This child of yours that I bear –
I know it –
Will be the death of me.

You will wash your face at the well.
You will turn your brow to the south.
I shall taste the last of your smile
In the brisk farewell of your mouth.
Sleep on, my love, sleep on.
Your child wakes in my womb.
    The child wakes.
    The branch breaks.
Come sunrise you'll be gone.

SCENE EIGHT
ENTER A DUCHESS

A hunting party in the forest. The Duchess has a hawk on her wrist. She sees Sancho and Don Quixote, and recognises them from her reading of Part One.

Duchess Tell me, sir. Am I mistaken, or is your master over there the celebrated Don Quixote de La Mancha?

Sancho Panza He is indeed – Don Quixote, formerly the Knight of the Sorrowful Countenance and now, for his bravery, known as the Knight of the Lions.

Duchess The Knight of the Lions! Did he fight with such savage beasts?

Sancho Panza He did so, and won hands down in single combat. There was no contest, frankly. Not even close.

Duchess I see. A Hercules!

Sancho Panza Not a Hercules, Your Grace. My master informs me that Hercules was sometimes effeminate. He wore women's clothes.

Duchess And you, my friend. You are the celebrated Sancho Panza.

Sancho Panza At your service, madam.

Duchess Go tell your master that my husband, the Duke, and I would be delighted to entertain him in our palace, which is not far from here. We have read much of his exploits, and have admired his courage and vision in seeking to revive the age of chivalry.

Sancho Panza I will tell him that. I'm sure it will give him much pleasure.

Sancho leaves. The Duchess addresses her attendants.

Duchess Go ahead to the Duke, and tell him we have found the mad knight, Don Quixote, and his fat squire, wandering in the forest. I have invited them to our home. We shall have some fun with them. The Duke will know what to do. I haven't got any more.

Courtly music as the courtiers of the palace roll out the red carpet for Don Quixote and Sancho Panza.

Chorus
I see their tents pitched far on the horizon.
I hear their horses thunder across the plain.
Where are the kings and where the lords in waiting?
Bring back the age of chivalry to Spain.
Where are the kings and where the lords in waiting?
Bring back the age of chivalry to Spain.

When the two men arrive in the palace courtyard, two women appear and throw a red mantle over Don Quixote, and sprinkle him with 'whole bottles of sweet-scented waters'.

Duke Welcome to the flower of chivalry. Welcome, Don Quixote de La Mancha!

Don Quixote it is strange. Until today I never quite believed that I was indeed a knight errant. But look at this.

Duke We welcome you and honour your Lady Dulcinea del Toboso.

Don Quixote Alas my lady suffers under a terrible enchantment, my lord. She has been transformed into a poor peasant girl.

Duke Transformed?

Don Quixote By a wizard.

Duchess Sancho, have you witnessed this enchantment?

Sancho Panza Yes, it was me who hit upon her enchantment in fact . . .

Duke Then we must find a way to release her. Bring forth Clavileno.

Enter four elaborately dressed Courtiers bearing a wooden horse. In the commotion the Duchess takes Sancho downstage.

Duchess You look reticent, Sancho

Sancho Panza I made him believe she was enchanted but there's no more truth in it than the story of a cock and a bull.

Duchess My dear Sancho Panza, here we have our own wizards who love us and tell us all that passes in the world. While you thought you were deceiving him, honest Sancho, you were in fact being deceived.

Courtier Let him who has the courage to do so mount this machine, for this is the flying horse Clavileno.

Sancho Panza You can count me out. I was not born to fly. I don't have the courage, and as it happens I am not a knight.

Courtier Let the knight mount the horse, and let the squire, if there be a squire, get up behind him, and trust in the powers of the valorous giant Malambruno, whose powerful magic will lift the enchantment from the Lady Dulcinea. Clavileno will bear them through the air to where Malambruno awaits them. No sword nor malice shall touch them. But the altitude of the flight, and the sublimity of their journey, may make their heads swim. Therefore their eyes should be covered, and should remain covered, until the neighing of the horse, which marks the journey's end.

Don Quixote Sancho, let's do it. Immortality awaits. But it will not wait forever

Sancho Panza Thank you, but no. To put on a blindfold and fly though the air requires courage. Expecting that sort of courage from me is like looking for pears on an elm tree.

Duke Sancho, you mentioned an island – you want to govern an island. And as it happens I have just the sort of island that might suit. But you know – no one in this fallen world receives an office of such value without paying something for it.

Sancho Panza You mean a bribe.

Duke A bribe if you will. A sweetener. A douceur. And what I expect for this island of mine is that you first accompany your illustrious master on his trip through the skies. You will find, Don Quixote, a wooden peg attached to the horse's head. Turn it upwards, the horse rises in the air. Turn it the other way, and it floats back to the ground. And now the necessary blindfold.

Don Quixote is blindfolded.

Don Quixote Now Sancho, duty calls.

Very nervously, Sancho climbs on to the horse to sit behind Don Quixote.

Hold on while I turn the peg.

The Courtiers have rattles to suggest the working of a wooden mechanism, and bellows to imitate the wind.

Courtiers
Valorous knight,
And you his squire,
Sit close and sit tight
As you fly higher.

Oh but beware
As you fly higher
The region of air –
The region of fire.
Oh but beware
The region of fire!

Don Quixote Can you not squeeze me quite so hard, Sancho? I don't see what you're so worried about. The flight is so smooth it's almost as if we hadn't moved.

A Courtier shakes the horse.

A little turbulence. Nothing to worry about.

Sancho Panza The wind is so strong it's as if a thousand pairs of bellows were blowing at me.

Don Quixote Now we have reached the second region of the air, where hail and snow are formed. Thunder and lightning are engendered in the third. At this rate we shall soon reach the region of fire, and I'm not quite sure how to work this mechanism so as to avoid being scorched.

The Courtiers wave lighted rags at the pair.

Sancho Panza That's it. That's the place of fire. We're going to be incinerated like a pair of heretics.

Don Quixote I shall turn the peg now. We're going down.

The Duke and Duchess arrange for fireworks to be let off. The horse collapses, bringing Don Quixote and Sancho 'back to earth'.

Remarkable. The machine has returned to the exact spot from when we ascended. Like an old horse returning to its stable.

Duke Congratulations, both of you. You have passed the test and lifted the enchantment from your beloved Lady Dulcinea. And now, Sancho, it is time to go to your island. Bid farewell to your master.

Sancho Panza Farewell?

Duke This is where your paths divide.

Don Quixote *and* **Sancho Panza** I hadn't thought about that.

They are both thunderstruck.

Duke Governing an island can be a lonely business. But I have every confidence in you. Meanwhile, Don Quixote, you will be shown to your room. You must be tired after your journey.

Don Quixote Goodbye, Sancho.

Sancho Panza Goodbye, master.

SCENE NINE
SANCHO'S GOVERNMENT

In his capacity as governor, Sancho Panza is welcomed to the city of Barataria. Bells are rung. Crowds throng the streets. He is brought to the governor's palace, where he stops at an inscription on the wall.

Sancho Panza Friend, tell me what is written up there on the wall.

Steward It says, 'On this day, Señor Don Sancho Panza took possession of this island, and long may he enjoy it.'

Sancho Panza And who is this Don Sancho they refer to?

Steward Why, to Your Lordship.

Sancho Panza Take notice, brother, Don does not belong to me, nor ever did to any of my family. I am called plain Sancho Panza. My father was a Sancho, and my grandfather a Sancho, and they were all plain Panzas. I fancy there are more dons than stones on this island. If my government lasts four days, I may weed out these dons. They are as troublesome as gnats. Well, I've spent all morning listening to their cases. Now I must eat. Aha!

The waiters bring dishes of food and place a bib around Sancho Panza's neck. A Physician stands at his side. Every time Sancho reaches for a dish, the Physician, using a tool like a croupier's rake, pushes the food beyond Sancho's reach.

Excuse me. Is this some kind of game?

Physician My Lord, I am a physician, and I have an appointed salary on this island. I study the governor's constitution night and day, letting him eat what I think is most suitable for him, and removing what I imagine will do him harm.

Sancho Panza What you imagine!

Physician That fruit, for instance, would be too moist and would hurt your stomach, and that meat dish is far, far too spicy and would increase your thirst. Anyone who drinks too much consumes the radical moisture in which life consists.

Sancho Panza Well then, pass me that dish of partridges. I've had a long morning's work governing, and I need food.

Physician My Lord Governor, as long as there is breath in this body, not a single morsel of partridge shall pass your lips.

Sancho Panza Why not?

Physician Hippocrates says: *Omnis saturatio mala, perdicis autem pessima.* 'All saturation is bad, but that of the partridge is the worst of all.' I simply couldn't take the risk.

Sancho Panza Rabbit?

Physician Tsk. Tsk.

Sancho Panza Veal then. What's that?

A great din of trumpets and drums, ringing of bells, voices raised.

Duke Arm, arm yourself, My Lord Governor. A huge number of enemies have invaded the island

Sancho Panza What do you mean, arm myself? I don't know the first thing about arms.

Duke Your island needs you.

Sancho Panza No, listen, if you want an expert on arms, my old master Don Quixote is the man. He would take on these enemies you talk about, just like that. It's just the kind of challenge he enjoys. Me, I'm a peaceable sort of –

Duke What is this, cowardice? You are the governor. Everything depends on you.

They tie two huge breastplates to his front and back, so he looks like a tortoise and can hardly move. Shouts of command are passed along the line:

Guard the postern. Guard the postern.

Scaling ladders, this way. Scaling ladders this way. *etc.*

Cauldrons of resin, cauldrons of resin *etc.*

Pour the boiling pitch, pour the boiling pitch.

Bring on the burning oil, burning oil, burning oil.

Man the barricades, man the barricades, *etc.*

Sancho Panza I wish I'd never seen this cursed island. I wish I was out of here.

Change of tone among the crowd.

Crowd Victory, victory. The enemy is routed. Long live General Panza. Long live the invincible Sancho Panza!

Sancho Panza Get me out of this armour and give way. Give way, gentlemen, and let me return to my ancient liberty. I was not born to be a governor, or to defend islands from the assaults of enemies. I know how to plough and dig, to dress vines and prune an orchard. I'd rather take a bellyful of my own poor gazpacho, than be humiliated by an impertinent physician. Now, where is Dapple? Dapple! Come here, Dapple, my loyal friend. When I kept company with you, I was a happy man. Go tell the Duke on my behalf: I came here without a penny to my name, and I will leave here penniless, unlike most governors.

Physician Sir, you can eat whatever you want. I will not stop you.

Sancho Panza My mind is made up. I am of the race of the Panzas. We are a stubborn lot. Now, Dapple, let's go.

Duchess You look sad, Don Quixote. You are missing your squire, perhaps. But there are plenty of men and women here at court to wait on you.

Don Quixote Thank you, madam, but I would rather wait upon myself tonight, and stay in my room.

Duchess No, no. I shall send you four of my most beautiful damsels.

Don Quixote Be kind enough to let me be alone. Let me look after myself. Let me keep a wall between my passions and my modesty. I would sooner go to bed in my clothes than let anybody help undress me.

Duchess Enough, enough. I will give orders that not so much as a fly shall enter your chamber, much less a damsel. Good night, Don Quixote.

Don Quixote Good night, madam.
   Sancho? Sancho?
   I hadn't thought about that. Sancho goes off to his island, to his reward, and I am left in my comfortable palace apartment . . . alone. When was I last alone? I wonder. For there was always somebody – my niece – I wonder what she's doing now, mending some garment I suppose – the housekeeper, picking stones out of the lentils – that boy, not very bright, whittling a stick. There is always somebody. But to be alone – oh, what is going on?

   A sackful of cats is emptied into the room through the window.

Cats! No! Out! Out! Begone!

   The cats run around the room. Don Quixote draws his sword and chases them off.

78

I am the Knight of the Lions, and yet I am still afraid of cats. And what is this? Am I afraid to be alone?

The Watcher in the Square

I wake in the night with a start.
A log settles in the grate.
And what was that?
A cat? A rat?
I hate them both with all my heart.
What business have they being up so late?

And what about that man
On the dark side of the square?
What harm has he
In mind for me?
What dark malevolent plan?
What business has he standing watching there?

The night is on the tiles.
A mood settles on the moon.
It gives the faintest of all watery smiles.
It will be going soon.

But when the smile is gone
And darkness has its day
The watcher at my window will watch on.
He will not slip away.

Though I take the forest track
Or ride the mountain trail,
I can never shake the watcher off my back,
The wizard off my tail.

In the stable lantern's soot,
In the soft step on the stair,
I shall glimpse the eye, I'll waken to the foot
Of the watcher in the square.

(*He begins to undress.*) These stocking of mine have quite disintegrated. They are like a spider's web, or a lattice

79

window. If I had the silk, I would darn them myself. (*Puts out the candles.*) How hot the night is!

Altisidora Don't ask me to sing, Emerencia. Ever since this stranger came to the castle, and my eyes beheld him, I have been too sad to sing. (*Strikes a few chords on the harp and sings.*) O woe, woe! . . . You see, it's hopeless.

Emerencia You love the Knight of the Green Stockings! Poor Altisidora!

They are suppressing their giggles.

Altisidora The knock-kneed Knight of the Green Laddered Stockings. The Knight of the Brass Barber's Basin! . . . Yes. Passionately. One glimpse of him and my knees turn to jelly – *jelly*, I tell you. I wobble uncontrollably.

Emerencia points to the open casement where Don Quixote is eavesdropping.

Emerencia You wobble. Have you confessed your passion?

Altisidora It's no use. He will not listen to my song. He's probably stretched out on his bed, lost in his dreams of romance, while here I languish, under his very nose. Men like that stride through the world leaving a trail of victims in their wake, quite unaware of the havoc they have caused among our sex.

Don Quixote affects a sneeze, in order to let them know he's there.

He hears me. Maybe he melts

Don Quixote I must not melt. I may not love you, Altisidora. I belong to Lady Dulcinea and to her alone. Roasted or boiled, Dulcinea's I must be.

Altisidora Roasted or boiled?

Don Quixote This castle is too full of adventure and intrigue. I fear for my chastity. Tomorrow I shall take my leave of the Duke and the Duchess.

SCENE ELEVEN
DON QUIXOTE REUNITED WITH SANCHO PANZA

Sancho and Dapple are on the forest track.

Sancho Panza Beaten, bruised, humiliated, mocked and lost. I wonder where I am.
  Oh no!

They fall into a pit, something like an old quarry.

Oh no, Dapple, I'm stuck. And now I shall starve to death. Oh Dapple, Dapple.

Dapple starts braying – a sad, long series of notes. Elsewhere in the forest, Don Quixote and Rosinante pause in their journey.

Don Quixote I know that bray! You hear that, Rosinante?

Rosinante neighs, louder than we have heard hitherto, and Dapple brays back in the distance.

It is strange. I thought for certain that Sancho was miles away, governing his island. Yet here is Dapple, braying his head off. Something is wrong. Maybe Sancho is dead.

Sancho Panza (*from the pit*) Ho there. Is there any Christian or charitable gentleman hears me?

Don Quixote Who is down there? Who is calling?

Sancho Panza It's me, Sancho.

Don Quixote He's dead, and his soul is doing penance for its sins.

If you are a soul in purgatory, let me know what I can do for you. If you are my squire, Sancho Panza, and happen to be dead, and if through God's mercy you are in Purgatory, our Holy Mother the Roman Catholic Church has prayers and supplications to deliver you from the pains you are in. I'll have the priest say mass for you when I get home.

Sancho Panza I am your squire Sancho Panza, and I was never dead in all the days of my life.

Don Quixote My dear fellow, it *is* you. Here, let me help you out. I thought you were governing that island of yours.

Sancho Panza And I thought you were being entertained by the Duke and Duchess.

Don Quixote To tell the truth, I had enough entertainment. I began to suspect that temptation was being deliberately put in my way, and I feared for my chastity. Wait! What is that?

Sancho Panza A funeral procession.

Don Quixote In the thick of the forest?

Sancho Panza A beautiful young woman. But if she died by her own hand . . .

Don Quixote It is Altisidora.

Mourners Weep for Altisidora. Weep for Altisidora. She died for love. She loved the stranger knight, but he was cruel and rejected her advances.

Don Quixote They are talking about me!

Mourners Where is the cruel knight and his heartless squire? Let them come to the grave of the victim of love. Weep for Altisidora! Weep for Altisidora! Kneel at her feet and weep.

Don Quixote Poor Altisidora. I never knew.

Altisidora sits up on the bier.

Altisidora Ha-ha-ha. It is the Knight of the Green Laddered Stockings! And did you think that I had killed myself for love of you – for you, the Knight of the Cats? You poor, sweet deluded man.

The Mourners burst into laughter and disperse.
Altisidora runs off with them.

Don Quixote That kind of thing is hard to credit. But we seem to have been living in a cruel kingdom. Is Dapple recovered? Yes? Let's be on our way.

Sancho Panza The world is a rough place, it seems.

Don Quixote
Love is a torment,
Love's a little urchin.
All the authorities
Warn us to beware.

He has a bow and
Yes, he has an arrow
To wound you
Or trap you in his snare.

SCENE TWELVE
THE DEFEAT OF DON QUIXOTE

Enter Samson Carrasco in full armour.

Samson Carrasco Illustrious knight, Don Quixote of La Mancha, I am the Knight of the White Moon, and I come to try the strength of your arm, to make you know and confess that my mistress, whoever she may be, is more beautiful than your Dulcinea del Toboso. Confess the truth of this now, and you will save me the trouble of taking your life. But if you fight and are vanquished by me – as vanquished you shall surely be – and if by chance I spare your wretched life, the satisfaction I shall expect is that you lay aside your arms, retire to your house for one year, where you shall live without setting hand to your sword, in profound peace and profitable repose. But if you vanquish me, my head shall lie at your mercy, the spoils of my horse and arms shall be yours, and the fame of my exploits shall be transferred from me to you.

Don Quixote Knight of the White Moon, I dare swear you never saw the illustrious Lady Dulcinea, for if you had seen her you would never have undertaken this challenge. I do not say you lie, only that you are mistaken. You must know that life is a trifle to me. Life is a bauble.

Sancho Panza I don't like the sound of this. I don't like this at all.

Don Quixote But honour is neither a trifle nor a bauble.

Sancho Panza Master, could I have a word with you? Something's cropped up.

Don Quixote Be quiet, Sancho. Knight, I accept your challenge and all your conditions but one. I do not know what your exploits are, or even if you have any. But I can do without your glory. Take whichever part of the field you please, and may Saint Peter give his blessing. And remember, if this goes ill with me . . . no intermeddling.

Sancho Panza I shall remember. I may not so much as lift a finger in your defence.

Don Quixote Now Sancho, my lance.

Samson Carrasco Have at you –

> *The two knights fight. Samson manages to unseat Don Quixote.*

Knight, you are vanquished and a dead man –

Sancho Panza No, no! Have pity! He didn't mean it . . .

Don Quixote Sancho, hold your tongue.

Samson Carrasco – unless you submit to the conditions of my challenge.

Don Quixote Lady Dulcinea del Toboso is the most beautiful woman in the world, and I the most unfortunate knight. Take my life. Take it. Go ahead. Push your lance in here.

Sancho Panza No, don't listen to him. He's upset. Have mercy on my –

Don Quixote *and* **Samson Carrasco** Sancho, shut up.

Samson Carrasco Well then, let the fame of Dulcinea live on. But I am still entitled to my satisfaction, which is that the great Don Quixote retire home for a year, and give up his adventures forthwith.

Sancho Panza I wouldn't pay any attention to him, personally. I mean, what right has he to –

Don Quixote I am a true knight and I shall obey you, whoever you may be. Sancho, help me off with my armour. I shall not be needing it. And look to Rosinante.

Samson Carrasco Lay down your sword.

Sancho Panza This is a dream. I seem to recognise that voice.

Don Quixote This is no dream, Sancho. This is defeat. But do not look so crestfallen, my dear friend. I am not the first knight to suffer defeat in battle.

Samson watches them as they depart. He removes his helmet.

Samson Carrasco No, not the first. The last, maybe.

Go Home, Old Man

Go home, old man. Your fighting days are over.
I dealt you your last wound. It's not so deep.
Go nurse your pride and you shall soon recover
And time will heal your shame. Go home and sleep.

Cold by the hearth or in the heat of battle,
Death comes to summon one and summon all –
The Pope from his prayer, the cowherd from his cattle.
There's not a man on earth who can ignore his call.

Go home, old man. Your fighting days are over.
You gave it to me then. The pain was sharp and deep.
A hero once, a warrior, madman, lover,
Go slumber by your hearth. Go home and sleep.

SCENE THIRTEEN
THE DEATHBED

Outside the house of Don Quixote. Sancho Panza and the Boy, who is strumming on a guitar.

Boy What was that song you used to sing, Sancho, about the raven in the tree?

Sancho Panza I can't remember.

Boy There was a King of England, who turned into a raven.

Sancho Panza Oh, and flew all the way to Spain. What was that song? He saw a knight beneath a tree. I haven't thought about it for –

Boy Did you ever visit England, Sancho, in your adventures?

Sancho Panza England . . . Yes and no . . . No.

Boy I am not dead . . .

Sancho Panza
 I am not dead,
 The raven said,
 I shall be king again.

Boy
 But you shall die,
 And you shall lie . . .

Housekeeper (*indoors*) Shhh. For Shame. Have you no respect?

A pause. Then the boy quietly resumes his strumming.

Boy They say the old man hasn't long to go.

Sancho Panza Don't you believe them. He's tough.

Boy And he's remembered you in his will.

Sancho Panza Naturally, one would expect a man in his position . . . not to forget certain key figures, irreplaceable friends and colleagues. I'm not expecting anything, of course.

Teresa Panza comes out of the house.

Teresa Panza What's the matter with you? Are you going to come in and pay your last respects? You're not afraid, are you?

Sancho Panza I am not! How could you say that after everything I've . . .

Teresa Panza You never could bear to see death. And now your beloved master is dying, you should be at his bedside.

Sancho Panza He's not dying, I tell you. He's as tough as old boots.

Teresa Panza Well, if he's not dying, you've got nothing to worry about, have you?

Sancho Panza I didn't say I was worried. Ow! Let go of my ear.

Voice of Don Quixote Is that you, Sancho? Come in. Come in.

Sancho is propelled into the room by Teresa. Everybody else is already assembled around the bedside.

Sancho Panza You sent for me, Don Quixote.

Don Quixote My dear Sancho, I did indeed, and the first things I must tell you is that I am no longer Don Quixote de La Mancha.

Sancho Panza Master –

Don Quixote No, hear me out. I wanted to tell you myself, for I owe you an apology. I am no longer Don Quixote. I am no longer mad. I am – no, listen to me – I am plain Alonso Quixano –

Sancho Panza Plain!

Don Quixote Plain Alonso Quixano. I am the sworn foe of all the writers of romances. All the histories of knight-errantry are odious and profane to me. I realise my folly now. Through the mercy of God, Sancho, I detest and abhor them. Through the mercy of God! The second thing I must tell you is that I am dying. I am not long for this world.

Sancho Panza No. That's not –

Don Quixote A man must not trifle with his soul, Sancho. I feel the hand of death upon me. I feel I have one foot already in the stirrup.

Sancho Panza Don't say such things.

Don Quixote Forgive me, Sancho. Forgive me. I was quite irresponsible and made you believe, as indeed I did myself, that there had once been, and were still, knights errant in the world. That was pure madness.

Sancho Panza Oh sir, dear sir, do not die. Take my advice and live for many years. The greatest madness a man can commit in this life is to allow himself to die without anybody killing him. Do not be lazy, sir. Get up. Get out of bed and face the world. Let us dress up like shepherds and go out into the fields and play on our pipes and – who knows – maybe behind some bush or other we may startle the lady Dulcinea, and she will flap up like some magnificent pheasant, free from the enchanter's spell.

But if you really are dying – if you are dying for grief at being vanquished – lay the blame on me. Tell them it was my fault for not fixing Rosinante's saddle properly. Besides, you must have read in your books, it is quite a common thing for one knight to unhorse another. It happens all the time. That's the way it goes, in chivalry: one day you're at the top of the tree, the next you're on your arse in the mud.

Niece That's true, Uncle.

Samson Carrasco Yes, sir, that's true. What Sancho says is true.

Sancho Panza I know that voice. Of course I know that voice. It was you all along. It was you! It was all of you conspired against him.

Don Quixote Gentlemen, let us proceed fairly and softly. Don't go looking for this year's birds in last year's nests. I was mad then. Now I am sober. Let my unfeigned repentance, and my sincerity, restore me to the esteem, to the love you once had for me.

Farewell, Sancho. Now, priest . . .

The Priest and the household gather around the bed.

Sancho Panza No. No.

The scene is frozen. Only Sancho can move. He gives the Epilogue.

Epilogue

Do not repent. We are not born for such repentance.
Do not berate your living self in death.
No word from you will mitigate the sentence
And there are better uses for your last breath.

There is a way to go – in what direction?
There is a stream to ford – who knows how wide?
There is a cave, and in that cave a question.
Climb to that cave mouth high up the mountainside.

This white path disappearing among the hills,
This donkey track, this narrow place to walk,
Where we enjoy our victories and our spills,
This life is but a tailor's mark in chalk.

This line of dust on cloth, this slash for a sleeve
Is what is left of our endeavour now.
Do not denounce this dust. Take a proud leave.
Wake, master, wake. Stand firm and take your bow.

Sancho leads Don Quixote to take his bow. Later the company dances a Seguidilla Manchega.

Finis.